banned

And I must go with stone feet
Down the staircase of flesh
To where in a shuddering embrace
My toppling opposites commit
The obscene, the unforgivable rape.

From Ern Malley's poem 'Sweet William'. Deemed indecent, Adelaide 1944.

Tales from
the bizarre
history of
Australian
obscenity

# banned

James Cockington

ABC
Books

Published by ABC Books for the
AUSTRALIAN BROADCASTING CORPORATION
GPO Box 9994 Sydney NSW 2001

*First published in June 2005*

National Library of Australia Cataloguing-in-publication entry:
Cockington, James, 1952– .
   Banned: tales from the bizarre history of Australian obscenity.

   ISBN 978-0-7333-1502-2

   1. Australia—Social life and customs—20th century.
   I. Australian Broadcasting Corporation.  II. Title.

994.04

Cover image: Photograph of Moira Claux by Max Dupain, circa 1950.
   Courtesy of Moira Claux and Jill White, keeper of the Max Dupain archive.
   Back cover images: top – sideshow alley strip-tease; middle – nudist magazine circa 1950;
   bottom – image from a 1935 edition of *Health and Physical Culture* magazine.
*Designed by saso content & design pty ltd*
*Set in Utopia 11pt on 16pt leading by saso content & design pty ltd*
*Colour reproduction by Graphic Print Group, Adelaide*

# Contents

# Great moments in obscenity

1855    Lola Montez performs her infamous Spider Dance in Sydney, Melbourne and Ballarat. She horse-whips a newspaper editor who dares to describe her act as 'not only shameful but indecent'.

1888    The Ballarat Art Gallery buys *Ajax* and *Cassandra*, the painting that inspires the young Norman Lindsay to a career in erotica.

1902    William Gocher, a local newspaper editor, challenges the prevailing law by bathing in daylight hours on Manly Beach. He is not arrested, thus starting the craze for beach culture.

1908    Marrickville-born Annette Kellerman is arrested in Boston for indecent exposure after wearing a pair of 'boy's' bathers.

1911    William James Chidley, wearing a Grecian tunic, is jailed for revealing *The Answer*.

1917    The first Australian Film Censor is appointed in Melbourne.

1920s   The decade in which Australia's oldest-surviving porn movie is thought to have been made. By whom remains a mystery. The movie is now in the possession of ScreenSound, the government film and television archive based in Canberra.

1930    Poet Kenneth Slessor celebrates the disappearing swimsuit in his poem 'Backless Betty from Bondi'.

1935    *Man* magazine begins publication.

1936    The Earl of Beauchamp's former private secretary is divorced by his wife on grounds of his homosexual tendencies. As proof of his depravity, excerpts from D. H. Lawrence's banned books are read out in court.

1940    The Spooner Ban, named after a New South Wales politician, is finally repealed after a series of public protests. It is now legal for men to expose their chests on beaches.

1940s   According to showbiz legend, Mo (Roy Rene) becomes the first person to use the word FUCK on stage — 'how come every time I write F, you see K?'. He was never charged.

1972 'Number 96' brings nudity and homosexuality to prime time TV. The Box, the 1974 spin-off series, goes even further, showing the first televised lesbian kiss. Raunchiest of all is the 1975 'Alvin Purple' series on Aunty ABC.

1976 Graham Kennedy gets a red card for his 'crow call', uttered during a live advertisement for hairspray. He resigns from Channel Nine only to return, bluer than ever, on Ten's 'Blankety Blanks'.

1984 Nigel Thomson's painting, *Children's Rites*, which includes a depiction of an erect penis, is withdrawn from the Sulman Prize at the Art Gallery of NSW. One of the detractors, artist Judy Cassab, later explains: 'Although censorship in art is abhorrent, I couldn't defend this painting with its sado-masochistic connotations connected to child pornography'.

1990s Celebrity censorship. Footballer Andrew Ettingshausen sues over unauthorised photo of him in a shower is published in *HQ* magazine. Newsreader Ann Fulwood sues over a raunchy cartoon of her is published in *Penthouse* magazine. Both are successful.

1992 Doug Mulray's 'Naughtiest Home Videos' special on the Nine Network is pulled from air, allegedly by boss Kerry Packer. Segments to that point had included a couple seen in the background making love on the bonnet of a car. An estimated 80 per cent of complaints to the network were from people wanting to see the rest of the show.

2002 A DVD of the film *Ken Park* is confiscated by police at a 'protest screening' at Balmain. 'Personally I just wish they hadn't banned it because then we wouldn't have had to see it', jokes Jonathan Biggins on 'Critical Mass'.

2004 A young man is arrested after taking photos of topless women at Coogee beach with his mobile phone camera. He is fined $500 and is banned from any beach in the council area while in possession of photographic equipment.

2005 The NSW branch of the Parents and Citizens' Assocations attempts to prevent parents from taking photos of their own children at school swimming carnivals without gaining written permission first. This proposal is later rejected after public pressure.

# chapter **one**

# Beyond Victoriana

**A**t the top of the stairs of the majestic Ballarat Art Gallery lives *Ajax and Cassandra*, a grand opera of a painting by the little-known English artist Solomon J. Solomon. He painted this minor masterpiece when he was a mere 26 years old. The work was purchased by the gallery in 1888 and it has occupied this most prominent position in the building ever since.

Eleven feet high and six feet wide, *Ajax and Cassandra* shows the named couple in a gymnastic pose during the sacking of Troy. The legend tells us that Ajax raped the seeress Cassandra in the temple of Minerva, although Solomon's interpretation seems to indicate a more consensual relationship. It portrays a level of passion

*Ajax and Cassandra*: the painting that so inspired the young Norman Lindsay.

rarely seen in public in the Victorian period. Both figures are lightly covered by convenientlydraped fabric.

This painting would hardly raise an eyebrow these days but it plays an important role in any discussion of Australian censorship. When he was growing up in this region, Norman Lindsay, aged eight or nine, was taken to see this painting and it made such an impression on him that he remembered it all his life. This was his first contact with the nude figure and, as he recalled 80 years later in his autobiography, it 'consumed me with a dolorous conviction of the hopelessness of ever attaining such a perfection in art'.

The unlikely guru introducing the boy to the nude painting, and thereby to his life's passion, was his maternal grandfather, the Reverend Thomas Williams—'full-bearded, stern, uncompromising and steady-eyed, he had something of the gaunt and craggy splendour of an Old Testament prophet' according to John Hetherington's biography of Norman Lindsay, *The Embattled Olympian*.

As a missionary with the Wesleyan church, the Reverend Williams had spent 14 years in Fiji converting cannibals to Christianity—a process that included forcing the natives to wear clothes and restrain their passion for human meat. So it comes as a surprise to learn that Solomon's depiction of flesh and lust was his favourite work in the gallery. He went to great lengths to translate its meaning to young Norman. It was their custom to leave this pleasure until their final descent of the stairs.

It seems likely that this minister of one of the more puritan forms of religion also had the gene of eroticism in him. Norman Lindsay's mother told him, much later on in life, that as her father lay semi-conscious on his deathbed, he raved about the beautiful figures of the young native women he had seen as a missionary.

'Perhaps, after all, I owe something of my own adoration of the feminine image to those Fijian girls absorbed as memory-images by the Reverend Thomas in the days of his lusty manhood', writes Lindsay. The Reverend died before he was able to see his favourite

The citizens of Creswick stand proudly in front of their new post office in the 1890s. The Lindsay residence was a short walk away.

COURTESY OF CRESWICK HISTORICAL MUSEUM

grandson emerge as the most banned artist and writer in Australian history.

Norman Lindsay was born on 22 February 1879 in Creswick, a village about 15 miles from Ballarat. Once part of the Melbourne gold rush region, Creswick was now a sleepy, country town. The days of grog shops and prostitutes were fading memories when Lindsay was growing up, replaced by a solid conservatism that Lindsay railed against all his life.

Some of the symbols of the conservative era are still there, including the Post Office and Town Hall. Also there is the American Hotel, a reminder of the earlier, wilder period when its owner Thomas Anthony was one of several Americans to arrive in the town in search of a quick profit. His hotel was one of 14 in this town in the 1850s, all doing a roaring trade in drunkenness and debauchery.

This region has a noble tradition in debauch. Lola Montez, the cigar-smoking entertainer, born Eliza Gilbert in Limerick, Ireland, came to Ballarat in 1855 as part of her Australian theatrical tour. The highlight of her performance was the notorious Spider Dance, in which she shook her petticoats in an effort to dislodge a mock

VICTORIA THEATRE,
BALLARAT.

This New and Elegant Theatre WILL OPEN

On SATURDAY, Feb. 16,

1856, under the Management of

MR. JAMES CROSBY,

Late Manager of the Victoria Theatre, Sydney,
On which occasion that world-renowned Artist, MADAME

LOLA
MONTES

And Troupe, will have the honor of making their first appearance, supported by the

Best Company ever assembled on Ballarat!
Aided by New Scenery, Dresses, and Appointments.

TOP and BOTTOM: Lola Montez (sometimes spelt Montes) was the sensation of the Victorian goldfields.

spider which, at the end of the dance, she crushed daintily with her foot. In the process the audience of mainly men were given glances of Lola's allegedly shapely ankles and calves.

The Spider Dance was considered as scandalous then as a lap dance would be today and Henry Seekamp, editor of *The Ballarat Star*, was inspired to write a lengthy editorial on her scandalous life, describing her stage act as 'not only shameful but indecent'.

Lola demanded a public meeting with her critic at the United States Hotel and, in front of a crowd of invited guests, attacked Seekamp with a horse whip. They had an all-out brawl which resulted in the newspaper editor being dragged away minus some of his hair. Thanks to this inspired publicity, Lola played the rest of her Goldfields tour to packed houses. The diggers showed their appreciation by throwing fragments of gold onto the stage.

No doubt Lindsay would have approved of the Montez philosophy of life which she set out in her 1858 autobiography. 'Perhaps the noblest courage, after all, is to dare to meet one's own self—to sit down face to face with one's own life, and confront all those deeds which may have influenced the mind or manners of society, for good or evil.'

The days of Lola Montez and the Gold Rush were distant memories by the time Lindsay grew up in Lisnacrieve, the family home in Victoria Street, next to the Wesleyan church in which his grandfather had once preached. There was little stimulation to be found anywhere near here so he turned to creating his own and became a local legend through his skill in drawing pornography.

Lindsay's first contact with obscenity is recorded with nostalgic glee in his autobiography, *My Mask*.

'A friend of Lionel's had returned from the Grand Tour of Europe, bringing back with him some French postcards, designed in a key of the skittish pornographic, and those supplied subject-matter for some of my ribald drawings and saved me the nuisance of thinking up a gag of my own that could raise a laugh.'

Young Norman, estimated age 15, soon became locally famous for his sketched copies of these postcards. On a trip to the nearby Lal Lal Races, he was instructed to bring some along by an older acquaintance—'a dark Satanic lad with a base sense of humour'—to impress some girls he had invited. The facsimiles were passed around at lunch and produced the desired shocked giggles among the girls, one of whom, Flo, decided to keep them in her purse.

As in a melodrama, the purse was then stolen.

Flo reported the theft to a nearby detective. He found a convicted pickpocket in the crowd who was dragged over to be charged. It was only then that the victim realised her mistake. The stolen purse still had the pornographic postcards inside. Fortunately, the suspect didn't have the purse on him. She told the detective that she wanted to drop the charges.

Still the situation proved intolerable for Lindsay.

'The purse would be found', he recalls thinking. 'The draw-ings would come under the inspection by the law's censorious eye. They would be traced to me. I would be subjected to whatever penalty the law imposed on the production of works technically labelled obscene.'

That scenario never happened, although 75 years later he was still able to remember the personal purgatory he went through in the weeks following the theft. Neither purse nor pornography ever emerged, although Lindsay's dark Satanic friend constantly reminded him what would happen if it did.

'I don't suppose you'll get more than a couple of months quod for them', he suggested. Quod, slang for prison, must have brought immediate images of the ominous bluestone cell, with barred windows above head height, that still sits ominously next to the former Creswick Court House in Raglan Street. The cell was just a hundred yards from the Lindsay family home. He must have walked past it just about every day.

What this incident proves is that even in the twilight of Queen Victoria's puritanical reign, pornography was widely available in Australia and managed to travel as far overseas as Creswick. The official censorship of print material was a relatively new phenom-enon in Australia, with obscenity acts being passed in the various states and colonies between 1876 (Victoria) and 1902 (Western Australia). Books were the main focus. Porno postcards apparently still entered the country freely in sailors' pockets.

The first major seizure of books took place in July 1889 when Victorian Customs seized a shipment of 162 French novels, including Alphonse Daudet's *Sapho* and Guy de Maupassant's *A*

OPPOSITE: One of those dirty French postcards, in this case with a hint of lesbianism.

*Lady's Man.* This action was partly inspired by the imprisonment a year before of Alfred Vizetelly, publisher of the English translations of Emile Zola's works. Some of Zola's novels had already been confiscated by Victorian Customs in 1887.

Melbourne's *The Age* newspaper considered this a good thing, claiming that 'probably every sane person agrees that Zola is not only filthy but revolting, and that literature would lose very little if almost all the productions of the so-called realistic school … were burned on the pyre that consumes confiscated cigars at the Customs House'.

This was a relatively mild review compared to some. 'He eliminates all from men but the ape and the tiger', declared the *Fortnightly Review*. Only a few came to Zola's defence, notably Havelock Ellis and Henry James. No one in Australia was that brave.

These banned translations make an interesting moral barometer. In Zola's most famous work, *Nana*, the heroine—'the Venus of the gutter'—makes her first dramatic appearance on stage at the Theatre des Varieties. 'With quiet audacity, she appeared in her nakedness, certain of the sovereign power of her flesh. Some gauze enveloped her, but her rounded shoulders, her Amazonian bosom, her wide hips, which swayed to and fro voluptuously, her whole body, in fact, could be divined, nay, discerned, in all its foam-like whiteness of tint, beneath the slight fabric she wore. It was Venus rising from the waves, with no veil save her tresses. And when Nana lifted her arms, the golden hairs in her armpits were observable in the glare of the footlights.'

Later, Australian readers who secured a blackmarket copy of the banned novel would have witnessed one of the first descriptions of lesbian sex when the enigmatic Satin seduces the heroine. 'And, once in bed, she forthwith took Nana in her arms, and soothed and comforted her. She refused to hear Fontan's name mentioned again, and each time it recurred to her friend's lips, she stopped it with a kiss. Her lips pouted in pretty indignation, her hair lay loose about her, and her face glowed with tenderness and childlike beauty.'

This was hot stuff for the times but as the celebrated Australian historian Cyril Pearl has documented in his 1955 book, *The Girl with the Swansdown Seat*, much more obscene literature was available in the Victorian era for those who had the contacts. In Britain all the usual niche areas of sexuality were covered including homosexuality and lesbianism, bondage and discipline, fetishes and cross-dressing. Spanking was perhaps the strongest interest.

These subjects were also discussed openly by physician Professor Richard von Krafft-Ebing in his landmark 1886 work, *Psychopathia Sexualis*. This was a serious scientific treatise which made it exempt from censorship and, to prevent prurient interest, the more salacious details were originally printed in Latin. Still, those with a classical education could read, for the first time, case histories of 'the undersexed and the hypersexed, rapists, stranglers, rippers, stabbers, blood-sucking vampires and necrophiliacs, sadists who hurt their partners, masochists who thrilled at the sight of the whip, males in female clothes and females in male clothes, stuff-fetishists dominated by a shoe or a handkerchief, lovers of fur and velvet, slaves of scatology, defilers of statues, despoilers of children and animals' ... Not to forget the unfortunate gentleman whose only sexual stimulus was an apron.

There was also perversity in everyday life. Prostitution was rife in both Sydney and Melbourne, reaching a peak towards the middle of the nineteenth century when one scandal sheet, Bell's *Life of Sydney*, reported that 'the plague extends instead of being abated, and the most callous-hearted can scarcely fail to feel a shock, when viewing the immense crowd of females, most of them exceedingly young, who traverse the principal streets of the city, or haunt the theatrical entrances in quest of the bitter bread of sorrow, insult, and infamy!'

Brothels were prolific in Castlereagh, Druitt and College streets, even more so in outlying suburbs like Woolloomooloo where one entrepreneurial pimp, John Rushton, ran 20 establishments staffed by girls as young as 12. Street workers were even younger. Inspector Charles Harrison of the detective police, in his 1859 report to the select committee on the condition of the working classes in Sydney, told of a homeless nine-year-old girl working the Sussex Street beat. Acting on a tip-off he burst into a hovel, catching her in the act with a man at least 40 years old. The valiant Inspector Harrison struck the man a solid blow on the head and threw him down a flight of stairs, later explaining that 'as the man appeared to be seriously injured, I did not take him into custody'.

At the time brothels were only outnumbered in popularity by public-houses. Sydney had 400 in the central police district alone, or about one to every 112 inhabitants. Debauchery, real or imagined, also applied to those at the higher end of the social scale. Sir James Martin, New South Wales' Premier and Chief Justice, was a keen classicist who, as would Norman Lindsay half a century later, professed an affection for the ancient god Dionysus. Sir James erected many tributes to this most swinging of deities in the gardens of Clarens, his now-demolished waterfront estate at Potts Point. One of these, an exact replica of the *Choragic Monument of Lysicartes*, now sits on the lower lawn of Sydney's Botanic Gardens. Those with sharp eyes will see several figures performing in a Lindsay-esque manner near the top of the monument.

Another example of what might have been deemed as obscenity occurred in the Lindsays' own backyard, just over the fence from the Wesleyan church where the aforementioned Reverend Thomas Williams had once been minister.

Around the turn of the twentieth century (1902 according to one estimate), Norman Lindsay began to experiment with photography. He especially liked to set up theatrical group portraits, based on classical and literary references.

'Hot stuff going on over at the Lindsays'. Norman Lindsay first experimented with photography in 1902.

'The field was limitless—Lord Suckfist pleading before Pantagruel, a scene from a stage melodrama of the gaslight era, an episode from Petronius, or anything else that touched his fancy', writes John Hetherington. 'The kitchen garden of Lisnacrieve was a perfect setting for their tableaux. Small boys dragged themselves up and watched over the high board fence, then went away round-eyed to spread the word, "Hot stuff going on over at the Lindsays".'

In one surviving example of this hot stuff, Norman's brother Percy was snapped in the backyard at Creswick embracing a female friend, also naked except for some conveniently-draped fabric.

These photos may not be pornographic by today's standards but if they had been discovered at the time by the moral authorities, chances are Norman Lindsay would have been sent to prison for a lot longer than a few months.

Censorship in Australia became a national issue with the formation of the Federal Customs Act near the end of 1901. Three months before the act was proclaimed, Federal Customs officers decided to trial it by seizing another consignment—more dirty French novels—including translations of Balzac's *Droll Stories* and Paul de Kock's *Monsieur Dupont*.

The importer, George Robertson Proprietary, had the distinction of being the first of many that century to be charged under section 52 of the Copyright Act, which declared 'blasphemous, indecent or obscene works or articles' to be prohibited imports.

At the court case, three learned witnesses described these books as filth. Professor Miller of Melbourne University went further, adding: 'I felt I needed a bath [after reading them].' The magistrate was more temperate. He determined that regardless of his personal opinion, there seemed to be some evidence that the books were obscene under the meaning of the law. Without enthusiasm he fined George Robertson a minimal 25 pounds and awarded no costs. From its first application the law regarding obscenity proved to be unsatisfactory, even to magistrates. Those interested in the predominantly legal manifestations of censorship are requested to seek out a copy of Peter Coleman's delightful 1962 publication, *Obscenity, Blasphemy, Sedition* (reprinted in 2000 by Duffy & Snellgrove). Coleman is chiefly concerned with literature in his text.

Having now left Creswick, Norman Lindsay experienced his first official battle with the forces of censorship when he exhibited a pen drawing, *Pollice Verso*, at the Royal Art Society of New South Wales' Annual Exhibition in Sydney in September 1904. This work shows a man, possibly Christ, crucified on top of a hill. In the foreground is a mass of figures, mostly naked. Some are looking at the crucified figure with arms outstretched and thumbs pointed down. Many seeing the drawing interpreted it as a condemnation of Christ and a promotion for hedonism.

Lindsay himself later confirmed this in print.

'All through my work I have maintained that theme and that is the reason I was attacked, although the attack took the crude device of denouncing it as indecent and immoral, because I took the nude human body as my symbol of the freed human spirit of man.'

The critic for the *Sydney Morning Herald* denounced Lindsay for 'depicting only the bestial types of humanity'. Such reviews, plus several outraged letters to newspaper editors, ensured a steady flow of spectators to the exhibition, attracted to it in the words of John Hetherington: 'like sensation-seekers going to gape at a two-headed calf'.

The work somehow escaped being banned in Sydney and thanks to the controversy he was able to sell it, for the unheard-of price of 150 guineas, to the National Gallery of Victoria. When shown there in 1907 the response, from public and critics, was generally favourable.

'Yet a myth persists that *Pollice Verso* was loudly and stormily denounced in Melbourne, on moral and religious grounds', writes Hetherington, suggesting that the myth may have been inspired by Lindsay's own comments. If he hadn't already learnt the lesson back in Creswick, the artist now knew that negative publicity inevitably led to higher price tags. He encouraged controversy and even admitted that the regular bans of his work were to his ultimate advantage.

Hetherington takes this further in suggesting that one of Lindsay's pet theories was that attack was essential to all creative self-expression. 'He believed it tested the artist's endurance and forced on him a deeper understanding of the concept of life he was striving to define.' And, in the case of *Pollice Verso*, he even appears to have created attack where none existed.

# chapter **two**

# Taking the waters

**A**t the same time as Norman Lindsay was embarking on his love affair with the nude figure, it was still against the law in most parts of the country to bathe fully-clothed in public in daylight.

As early as the 1830s the New South Wales Government had passed The Bathing Act, stating in part 'that it shall be unlawful for any person to bathe near or within view of any public wharf, quay, bridge, street, road or other place of public resort within the limits

Nudity, for men, was the norm at the Figtree Baths in Sydney, 1872.

of any of the towns between six o'clock in the morning and eight in the evening'.

Similar laws were in place in Melbourne by 1841, with particular emphasis on the Yarra, in those days apparently suitable for swimming. Bathing was done privately in secluded beaches and rivers and in enclosed baths, but the thought of someone swimming, even fully clad, where they could be observed by those strolling on the esplanade was considered deeply obscene, and remained so until the turn of the twentieth century.

In the nineteenth century, women were only allowed to swim (the activity was popularly known as 'taking the waters') at segregated reserves like Mrs Esther Bigg's Baths at Woolloomooloo Bay or the Ben Bolt Baths near today's Royal Botanic Gardens in Sydney. Here, according to an 1840s report, 'the Ladies are safely secure from all intrusion and they can gambol unseen and unmolested'.

Not that there would have been much to see.

*Australian Etiquette*, a publication released in 1885, gave details of the appropriate attire for women.

'Flannel is the best material for a bathing costume, and grey is regarded as the most suitable colour. It may be trimmed with bright worsted braid. The best form is the loose sacque, or the yoke waist, both

Women were expected to take the waters dressed like this.

of them to be belted in, and falling about midway between the knee and ankle.' An oilskin cap and merino socks completed this monstrous outfit. The face, the neck, arms and legs from the calf downwards were the only sections of flesh exposed.

No equivalent male costume was mentioned. At this stage it was the custom for men to swim naked in private baths. Children also swam naked, which was a sticking point raised by the Inspector Charles Harrison in his aforementioned 1859 select committee report.

'I have frequently observed a number of children, ranging from infancy to 12 or 14 years of age, in a state of nudity, bathing at the different wharves leading out of Sussex Street', he noted, adding that these children were of both sexes. 'I believe it is intercourse of this kind which first breaks down the barrier of decency, deadens the sense of modesty, and leads to criminal intercourse between boys and girls whilst they are only children', Harrison concluded, adding that he had eye-witness reports from a Pyrmont Bridge toll receiver of 'criminal intercourse' taking place.

Possibly the first organised experiment in mixed bathing was conducted at the private Natatorium indoor pool in Pitt Street, Sydney, where the Sydney Dual Swimming Club held races for both sexes in 1892. Spectators, mostly male, crowded the gallery and one journalist noted that the women looked 'too natural' in their clinging jersey costumes.

There seems to have been a relaxation of the rules in the last decade of the nineteenth century and it was reported that many sinful folk of Sydney town were defiantly breaking curfews. At Manly Beach the 1830 law had been relaxed somewhat to allow bathing until 7 a.m. which was marked by the arrival of a man clanging a large dinner bell. This was later extended to 7.30 a.m.

The first to challenge the man with the bell was 43-year-old William Gocher, editor and publisher of the *Manly and North Sydney News*. On 1 October 1902, he announced in his own newspaper that the local by-law prohibiting swimming in daylight hours was absurd and he intended to defy the law by 'bounding in for a bathe' the next day. The next day was Sunday 2 October. After changing into his neck to knee costume at the Steyne Hotel, he crossed the Esplanade and entered the water. He was disappointed when nothing happened.

'No posse of police came flying down with drawn batons to the water's edge to yell out to me to come and be arrested', he wrote. 'There was no mighty concourse of citizens to cheer me as I came shooting in on No. 4 breaker, breathing salt spray and defiance. Outside my few bosom pals … the passing pedestrians took but a timid interest in my plunge for public liberty.'

After some more pre-publicity, Gocher performed the forbidden act again, and then once more. Finally, on this third attempt, the police arrived and, as intended, he was arrested. Later in his campaign Gocher interviewed Edmund Fosbery, the Inspector-General of Police, who told him that, despite the law, no magistrate would convict daylight bathers provided the men wore neck to knee costumes and the ladies did not expose their bosoms.

This assurance was not enough for Gocher, who continued his protest through the halls of Manly Council. On 2 November 1903, the council officially agreed to allow bathing in daylight hours provided everyone over the age of eight was covered from neck to knee. This allowed mixed bathing in public in daylight hours for the first time. Other Sydney councils followed suit and it was soon reported that surf bathing was now the chief pastime of decadent Sydneysiders.

But not without dissent.

In 1907, after receiving complaints from the public, the Mayor of Waverley, Mr R. C. Watkins, took a walk along the promenade at Bondi Beach and announced that he was shocked.

'What we saw was disgusting', he told the *Daily Telegraph*. 'Some of the surf-bathers are nothing but exhibitionists, putting on V trunks and exposing themselves, twisted into all shapes on the sand. Their garments after contact with the water show up the figure too prominently. Women are often worse than the men, putting on light gauzy material that clings when wet too much to be decent. But they won't continue it at Bondi, not so long as I am Mayor Watkins.'

The *Daily Telegraph* expressed the vain hope that 'no Draconian ordinances on the subject would be promulgated' but Mayor Watkins was already on the moral warpath, combining with the mayors of Manly and Randwick to decide that from now on all bathers should wear the following costumes ... 'a combination of a Guernsey with sleeves reaching to the elbow, and trouser legs reaching to the bend of the knees together with a skirt covering the figure below the hips.' This, the mayoral trifecta insisted, should be worn by both males and females.

Further laws forbad 'sunbathing i.e. loitering on the beach' and prevented any person in swimming costumes, even the ones specified, from mixing with a member of the general public unless the bather first puts on an 'overcoat, macintosh, or other sufficient wrapper or clothes'. Fines of up to ten pounds were set in place.

These rules were openly ridiculed in the press. 'To compel sensible men to dress in a pantomime dress, half-skirt, half-petticoat, is an insult to twentieth century civilization', wrote one outraged correspondent while another pointed out that lifesavers would be unable to do their duty while wearing a skirt.

A series of public protests followed, with surfers at Bondi parading while wearing embroidered ladies' petticoats, ballet skirts or sarongs made from curtain material. At Manly the parade was led by a man holding aloft a dead seagull on a pole. One protestor wore a doormat tied around his waist.

Approved swimming costumes, circa 1908, left a lot to the imagination.

Newspapers had a field day. 'Health and happiness for many thousands are considerations too important to be played with by stodgy individuals who have got beyond the age of enjoyment', concluded the *Sydney Mail*.

Eventually it was the compromise raised by Mr A. Relph of the Manly Surf Lifesaving Club that eventually took over. The Canadian costume consisted of a pair of knickers reaching halfway to the knee covered by a sleeveless guernsey top which extended to below the crotch. They were made from either cotton or a light-weight material known as stockinette which, as Mayor Watkins would have been shocked to observe, left little to the imagination when wet. These bathing suits allowed enough freedom for 'shooting the breakers' and aquaplaning—two of the more popular water sports of the period.

It seems Sydney was decades ahead of other states and other countries. In 1908, Marrickville-born swimmer Annette Kellerman

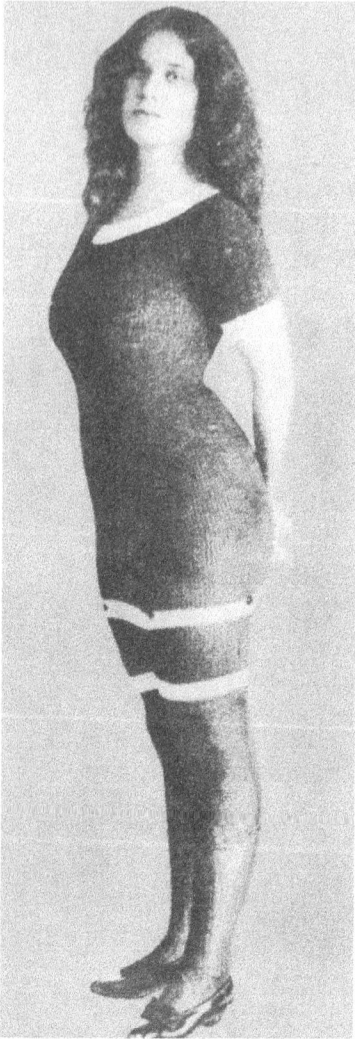

Winner of the 1911 Miss Venus competition, in a daringly brief costume for the time.

OPPOSITE: Saucy seaside postcards celebrated the rapidly diminishing swimsuit.

was arrested in Boston for wearing 'boy's bathers'—an abbreviated form of the Canadian costume.

There were no such shenanigans in more prudent Melbourne where bathing was either banned completely during daylight hours or only allowed when the sexes were strictly segregated. In 1908, while Sydneysiders were frolicking in their shocking stockinette costumes, a writer for Melbourne's *Punch* noted with envy that a suntan—'the browner the better'—was much admired north of the border. Another writer, for *The Lone Hand* magazine, observed that 'one of the strangest features of Sydney surf bathing to the stranger who hails from Presbyterian Victoria … is the casualness of the sexes on the beaches. They are partially naked but so unashamed as not to notice the fact.'

So unashamed that in 1911 the first Australian Venus Competition was held for young women wearing the new figure-enhancing swimsuits. This was perhaps our first beach beauty pageant. Prominent artists Julian Ashton and Sydney Ure Smith were two of the judges. The following year the Alhambra Theatre in George Street, Haymarket, was advertising continuous screenings, from 10 a.m. to 11 p.m., of the latest moving picture attraction, *Sirens of the*

"DO YOU THINK MY BATHING COSTUME SHOWS BAD TASTE?"
"NO. I THINK IT SHOWS VERY GOOD FORM!"

*Surf.* After each screening audience members were encouraged to vote for their favourite siren.

There was no such casualness south of the border. Mixed bathing was still a topic of moral debate and in 1912 Reverend Adamson, a Melbourne Methodist, declared that 'no modest woman can be associated with mixed bathing and no man who respects the opposite sex could take part in it'. He was responding to a report that men and women had been seen bathing together in the suburb of Moorabbin.

The Reverend had obviously done his research. He added, mysteriously, that 'if some of them who bathe could hear what is said about them they would be startled'.

At this time bathing of any persuasion was still banned in Melbourne on Sundays and other religious highlights like Good Friday and Christmas Day. On other days it was only permitted until 10 a.m. In 1912 South Melbourne became the first council in Melbourne to allow mixed bathing on their beaches, but the Sunday embargo remained and the sinful Sydney practice of 'sun bathing' was frowned upon.

St Kilda City Council even passed a by-law: 'Any person bathing shall on leaving the water forthwith resume ordinary clothing, and no person shall loiter save as far as necessary, to enable him or her to dress, run or walk in the vicinity in bathing costume, or without having resumed ordinary clothing'.

It's a matter for debate whether the predominant crime here was loitering, or being inappropriately attired for longer than necessary. One Sunday in 1914 a protest was held on St Kilda beach when a thousand bathing enthusiasts turned up en masse to defy the various laws, including the one forbidding mixed bathing. But it was bitterly cold and raining and only a few protesters braved the chill grey waters of Port Phillip Bay.

Melbourne's *Argus* newspaper considered sunbathing a dangerous social trend, one verging on pagan worship.

'The pastime has an astonishing charm for its devotees' ran a typical 1912 *Argus* editorial. 'Sometimes it becomes almost fanaticism. In these cases men and women can find time for nothing else. In their blind enthusiasm for the sun they are prepared to neglect such necessary formalities as the earning of a livelihood.'

People were actually convicted (and fined as much as five shillings) because of their blind enthusiasm for the sun. Melbourne beach enthusiasts had to wait until 18 January 1917 before they were allowed to swim, and sunbathe, in relative freedom. Even then, access to beaches on Sundays terminated promptly at 7 p.m.

Other sports were equally controlled by their own moral codes. Professional boxers were allowed to fight while stripped to the waist but women spectators were excluded from watching, or they were until the 1908 World Heavyweight Title staged at the Sydney Stadium at Rushcutters Bay. Jack Johnson, the first black world champion, beat Tommy Burns in a brutal encounter. Despite the ban against women—'when the claret begins flowing, prizefighting is no place for the gentler sex', wrote the stadium's then promoter Hugh D. McIntosh—at least one sneaked in. The wife of American novelist Jack London, in Australia as a sports reporter, wore male clothing to gain entry. She later pointed out the hypocrisy of the ban, mentioning that McIntosh encouraged women to pay to watch the two boxers in training sessions, while both sexes were allowed to watch the filmed highlights of the fight.

Jack Johnson, tall, shaven-headed and by all reports magnificently proportioned, knew the effect he had on white women and exploited it to the full. At his training sessions in Sydney he wore tights that accentuated his manhood (there were rumours that he padded his pouch, so to speak). He created a scandal in Sydney by inviting female admirers to visit him in his room at the Watson's

Bay Hotel, which they did in force, forming a queue at his door, according to folklore.

After this event future promoters of the Sydney Stadium, notably Snowy Baker and his brother Harald, encouraged women to attend nights of boxing and wrestling where most competitors fought 'semi-nude' according to the standards of the day. In the more liberated period after the First World War, this was seen as a fashionable and daring thing for women to do.

Each sport had its own dress regulations. Male tennis players had to wear long trousers and long-sleeved shirts in competition until the 1930s. Female competitors had to wear long skirts, long-sleeved tops and a hat. The All England Tennis and Croquet Club finally allowed women to wear shorts at Wimbledon on 16 May 1934.

# chapter **three**

# W. J. Chidley's answer

**W**hile early Australians generally dressed as if they were still living in London or Dublin, there were occasional attempts to introduce dress reform down under. The early part of the twentieth century saw a revival of interest in homeopathy and other aspects of natural living. One advocate was Broadbent and Sons, purveyors of medicinal herbs in Melbourne's Eastern Market—'all herbs guaranteed pure, fresh and true to name' claimed a sign above the premises. John Broadbent even produced a book, *The Australian Botanic Guide to Health*, which disputed the 'learned quackery' of modern medicine.

The current fashion for restrictive clothing was discussed within. Radical for the time, Broadbent suggested that healthy persons 'should

John Broadbent, seller of natural medicines, was an early advocate of dress reform.

be accustomed to wear but little clothing when indoors, and that perfectly loose about them.'

Or, to be specific: 'Too much cannot be said against compressing the chest, as is the custom of many females, who have thereby sacrificed themselves to the goddess Fashion, and we fear that many more must be sacrificed at the same shrine before the practice will be abandoned.'

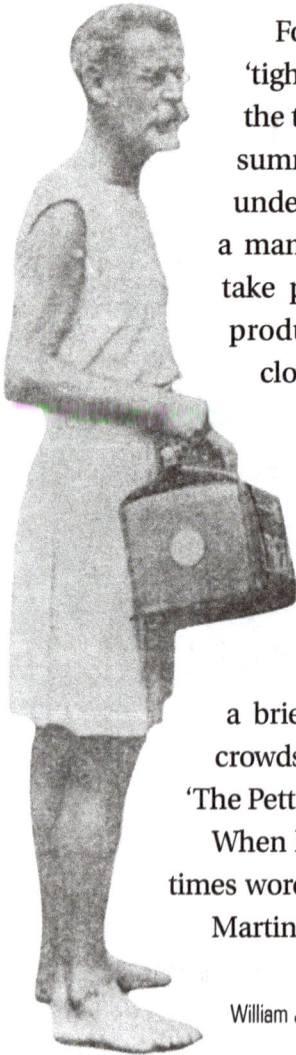

For the male of the species, the tip was to avoid 'tight bandages around the neck'—a reference to the then compulsory starched collars, worn even in summer with a three-piece tweed suit over long underwear. In contrast, Broadbent suggested that if a man were to live 'in accordance with his nature, take proper exercise in the open air, and thereby produce a free circulation of blood, but little clothing would be required'.

Only one man, it seems, dared take this advice literally.

Beginning his crusade in Adelaide in 1894, William James Chidley also argued that the style of dress adopted by most Australians was unhealthy and to prove it he began wandering the streets barefoot, wearing a brief Grecian-style tunic made of white silk. The crowds who inevitably followed him about called him 'The Petticoat Man' or 'Chidley, Wearer of Airy Garments'. When he first came to Sydney in 1911, Chidley sometimes wore a bathing costume while selling pamphlets in Martin Place or giving lectures in The Domain. When

William James Chidley wearing those airy garments.

asked about his choice of clothing by a reporter from Sydney's fledgling *The Sun* newspaper, Chidley said: 'I hate clothes. I feel warmer without them. I hoped to wear trunks, but the law would not permit it except if I wore something on top. Years ago I was told that I was a hopeless consumptive and was given two years to live. But my system of diet, fruit and nuts, coupled with my system of living, enables my body to deal with variations in temperature, however extreme, without inconvenience or discomfort. The sunbathers on our beaches are on the threshold of discovery. I must tell people what I have found to be right.'

Dress reform was just one of Chidley's social issues. He also advocated strict vegetarianism, eugenics and his own brand of sexology based upon a belief that the act of intercourse ('unnatural coition', as he called it) was the cause of most of the world's problems. He saw the male erection as a symbol of violence, as harmful to the man as the woman. These radical theories were elaborated upon in his pamphlet, *The Answer* (or *The World of Joy*). For one and sixpence each the public could obtain *The Answer* from Chidley's trademark fawn-coloured Gladstone bag.

Throughout his life Chidley was arrested and charged with various offences, including offensive behaviour, lecturing on a Sunday, obstructing traffic or, most frequently, selling an obscene publication. In Melbourne, copies of *The Answer* were ordered to be impounded and destroyed.

Typically, he decided to go to prison rather than pay the fine. Most considered Chidley a harmless eccentric but a few branded him a public nuisance, including those who ordered his arrest when a poster advertised that he would be giving a lecture—'to ladies only'—on 3 August 1912 at the King's Hall in Phillip Street. After a previous lecture for men, Chidley had been warned by police that a similar address to women would not be tolerated. The male lecture included warnings against masturbation and references to the non-violent sexual methods recommended by

Chidley, including a detailed analysis of a process he described as 'vaginal suction before male erection'.

Such details could not be openly discussed at a time when the New South Wales (NSW) Department of Public Instruction had just withdrawn Benjamin Franklin's autobiography from state schools after someone pointed out that Franklin made an obscure reference to the act of making love.

This time, when Chidley was taken to the court, he was charged with being insane and admitted to the Darlinghurst Reception House. On 7 August, after three doctors confirmed his insanity, Chidley was committed to Callan Park Mental Asylum.

Not everyone agreed with the doctors' verdict. In a letter to the editor, one correspondent argued: 'if a man's sanity is to be gauged by his writings, a number of authors should be in the safe keeping of the Government'.

Other supporters included the pioneering British sexologist Havelock Ellis (with whom Chidley corresponded) and the Dean of the Faculty of Medicine at Sydney University, Professor Anderson Stuart, who maintained that the subject of human sexuality was 'of social and ethical importance'. The Bishop of Tasmania and Professor Leurie of Melbourne also suggested that Chidley had at the very least a right to be heard.

Public meetings were held in Sydney at which enough money was raised to have

Professor Anderson Stuart supported Chidley's right to discuss sexual matters. 'I consider the subject to be of social and ethical importance.'

Chidley released on bond. Among the conditions of release were that he would not molest youths or children nor distribute circulars to women.

Upon his release Chidley resumed his street lectures and was arrested once again on 10 April 1913 and charged with selling an obscene publication (*The Answer*). This time Professor Anderson Stuart personally gave evidence on Chidley's behalf and even Judge Murray, in handing down a minimum fine, said he agreed with much that was in the publication.

For the next three years Chidley was a constant visitor to various mental institutions until he finally snapped while awaiting a further committal in the Darlinghurst Reception House courtroom. He managed to find some kerosene which he poured over himself before setting himself alight. He appeared to be recovering from the severe burns before he suddenly collapsed and died on 22 December 1916. Ironically, a group of his sympathisers decided to bury the noted dress reformer in a conventional dark suit rather than his preferred Grecian garments.

Shortly before he tried to commit suicide, W. J. Chidley had given his final public speech before the courtroom magistrate.

'I am a student of humanity, ethics, philosophy and psychology', Chidley claimed. 'I am the last of philosophers and my book is the answer to the pessimism of Schopenhauer and to all the questions of ethics.'

Having said this, he set himself on fire.

# chapter **four**

# Dirty dancing and stage kissing

'The first steps in a life of shame can be traced to the dance hall', said the Reverend Hugh Morris, a Presbyterian minister in Perth, in announcing a 1926 ban on dancing at church functions, with the exception of the Highland Fling which he conveniently described as a pastime, not a dance. Equally scandalous dance halls had opened up throughout the country, most shamefully in 1914 when the entrepreneur Hugh D. McIntosh imported 'the forbidden dance' to Australia.

In Sydney and Melbourne McIntosh introduced a concept known as the Tango Tea, at which the dance was demonstrated by 'six lovely girls in silken bloomer-cum-petticoat array, over which they wore corsets—suspenders loose and all a-jingle' according to the Melbourne *Punch*. 'A coat of black ninon, and boudoir cap; completed each of these undress toilettes, that created more sensation than the tango.' Those watching the demonstration were then urged to try it themselves.

Sydney embraced the new dance craze; Melbourne fought against it.

More than 700 citizens protested against the opening of the grand Palais de Dance in St Kilda after management announced that they intended to stage nightly displays of the wicked tango.

Such protestors were already being described as 'wowsers', a word that lexicographers have traced back to 1909 when it first appeared in the *London Daily News*. Three years later the Premier of Western Australia supplied a suitable local definition: 'a person who is more shocked at seeing two inches of underskirt than he would be at seeing a mountain of misery'.

Other targets for wowsers at the time included women smoking in public or taking spirits or intoxicating liquors. Or just about anything else.

During a lecture in 1917, Dr Michael Kelly, the Roman Catholic Archbishop of Sydney, added a few more to the list, including 'the feast, the dance, the theatre, the racecourse, the stadium, the field sports', warning that those who engaged in such pursuits … 'in a moment go down to hell'.

Sydney's Theatre Royal was the scene of some scandalous stage kissing.

The cinema didn't feature in this comprehensive list but others saw the moral danger. The dark nature of the activity was seen as an encouragement for young couples to engage in petting. Attempts were made to screen films with the lights on.

Any kiss in a public place was also seen as a ticket to purgatory, even more so when performed in the theatre.

'Stage Kisses'—'osculatory demonstrations in drama and comedy'—was the name of a scandalous gossip column in *Stage-land*, a magazine published in the 1920s by the J. C. Williamson

theatrical empire. Here the art of kissing was analysed as if it was a combat sport.

'In *Katja* there was a kiss that one remembers for the vigor of Warde Morgan and the contortion of Marie Burke, who bent back and back under the Russian onslaught', writes our anonymous expert.

Some stage kisses were verging on the pornographic.

'I have, in fact, watched ladies, whom I suspected of much experience, stir uneasily in their seats while Tondelayo's lips clung to young Langford's.'

The unease may have been partly explained by the fact that Tondelayo, the female lead in the play *White Cargo*, is described as 'a coloured coquette'. Although the part was played, with the aid of make-up, by milky-white English actress Ellen Pollock, this would have been one of the first depictions of inter-racial sexuality portrayed on the Australian stage.

The fact that this was allowed at all suggests that the Roaring Twenties were slightly more tolerant than the decade before, although inter-racial sexuality off the stage was still totally taboo.

In 1928 a troupe of 35 entertainers from Los Angeles known as The Coloured Idea was appearing at the Tivoli Theatre in Melbourne. Six of the musicians were picked up by the Criminal Investigation Bureau (CIB) during a 3 a.m. raid on a city flat. The six men were in the company of six white women. Although this was not against the law, the reaction of tabloid newspapers like the *Melbourne Truth*—'White Girls With Negro Lovers: Flappers,

OPPOSITE: While Dulcie Deamer claimed to be always adequately covered, Annette Kellerman was happy to pose in less.

Wine, Cocaine and Revels' screamed one headline—inspired a wave of outrage that forced the Minister for Immigration to have the entire troupe deported.

Elsewhere in *Stageland* are other indications of the gradual loosening of morals. Scattered throughout the magazine are photos of the latest stars of stage and screen posing in brief (for the time) bathing suits, plus gossipy tidbits from the scandalous world of the stage.

'That girl' said a Sydney manager, referring to a chorus beauty, 'is like the Tower of Pisa. She is always inclined, but she never falls.' Regardless of their morality, Tivoli Girls were seen as a small step above prostitution.

Dulcie Deamer emerged in the Roaring Twenties as the reigning Queen of Bohemia, a title she was given at a Sydney cafe called 'The Greek Club' when a 'black' magician named John Bennett placed a crown on her head. She dined out on this legend for the rest of her life, supported by a widely-published photo of her wearing a leopard skin costume at one of the notorious Artist's Balls which began in 1922.

An urban myth evolved that she liked to wander the streets of Kings Cross at night in her leopard skin (and nothing else) dancing wildly whenever the pagan spirits moved her. She became the symbol of the supposed decadence of the period. The reality was somewhat less exotic.

Later in life Dulcie confessed that her trademark leopard skin was only ever hired overnight from a fancy dress shop and, when wearing it to and from parties, was always modestly covered with an overcoat. She stressed that she was very adequately covered beneath the costume.

She also scoffed at suggestions that her life, or anyone else's in that period, was a blur of orgies, alcohol and cocaine. As a single mother with four kids to support, she spent most of her time grinding out the nine books and countless short stories she had published in her lifetime. The best known of these were tepid romances set in the tropics.

Despite Dulcie's claims of personal modesty, these Artist's Balls were apparently wild affairs. The poet Douglas Stewart recalls on one occasion seeing 'a girl wearing three tin pannikins and nothing else'.

It was customary for one or two policemen to sneak in, dressed not in plain-clothes but in fancy dress, to keep an eye on moral standards. At one year's function held at the Bondi Casino, a constable turned up dressed as a sheik. The disguise didn't work. The proprietor recognised the imposter and immediately pointed him out to everyone else in the room.

Despite Dulcie's disclaimer, the 1920s appear to have been roaring for some. On the shores of Lake Burley Griffin lies some graphic evidence. What is thought to be Australia's oldest surviving pornographic movie now sits in the air-conditioned vaults of the ScreenSound archive, 'on the third shelf at the end of the fifth row', reports Peter Luck in his book, *A Time to Remember*.

This movie has no credits and no sound but was obviously shot by a professional cameraman. Probably a newsreel crew on a slow day, suggests Luck. It took place in an area that looks like the Blue Mountains, west of Sydney. Some footage of a car, and the style of clothing worn (initially) by the participants, places it approximately in the early 1920s.

It breaks just about every rule set down by Sir Harry Wollaston, the first Commonwealth film censor, who mentioned a few of the more objectionable areas when he took up the position in 1917. These include: 'Indecent, suggestive or insufficient dress; embraces overstepping the limits of affection, or which would be contrary to propriety in ordinary life; nude figures, and positions of the actors which are suggestive of sexual passion or desire ...'

Why the film was made and where, if ever, it was screened remains a mystery. It might have done the illicit 'smoko' circuit, shown either

# X-BAZIN

*Famous French way of Removing Hair*

## Clean Limbed Beach Beauties

YOU will see them at all the beaches this Summer—attractive girls with arms, limbs and underarms free from disfiguring hair. Beauty is a matter of small details and X-BAZIN, the famous French hair-remover, is a wonderful aid to any girl who would look her best.

X-BAZIN is a harmless hair remover, daintily scented and pleasant to use. It leaves the skin white and satiny. Unlike shaving, it does not coarsen, darken or increase later growth.

X-BAZIN is sold everywhere in cream and powder form, both delicately perfumed

*Write for free sample to Sole Distributors for Australia and New Zealand.'*

FRAZER & BEST, LTD
Dept. 414 Box 261 Sydney, N.S.W.

ABOVE: Removal of body hair was first considered necessary in the roaring twenties.

BELOW: Along with the backless swimsuit came a fad for physical fitness.

in private homes or the locked backrooms of men's clubs. The film was handed in anonymously to the archive and can only be seen these days by serious researchers and the like. I must have qualified because I was given approval to see a video copy. It is as graphic as any X-rated movie made today, performed with enthusiasm by participants who were relaxed enough to show pleasure in their performances.

To see it is a curious experience, partly because we have been led to believe that nothing like this went on in our great-grandparents' time. It's like finding evidence of electricity being used in the seventeenth century. It shows that the sex act was openly enjoyed among at least one sector of Australian society and makes you wonder whether such pornographic movies were more common than the history books would have us believe.

What the Reverend Hugh Morris of Perth would have said about this is not recorded.

# chapter **five**

# **Backless Betty from Bondi**

**A**s early as the mid 1920s it was obvious that swimsuits were rapidly shrinking. This trend was subtly promoted by department stores like Farmer's in Sydney, which in 1926 advertised a range of American-style wool surf suits for women—'with larger arm holes'.

The larger the arm hole, the more skin was visible. Costumes were now half the size of what had been worn the previous decade. Thighs, arms, necks and even a hint of breast were exposed to the sun— and to the critical eye of roving moral guardians.

In 1925, members of Melbourne's Box Hill branch of the Women's Christian Temperance Union passed a resolution which placed skimpy swimsuits in the same category as alcohol and smoking. In part: 'We deplore the disgraceful exhibition of

An early advocate of the nude cult poses for a 1935 edition of *Health and Physical Culture* magazine.

men and women, who not only parade our beaches in a semi-nude state, but pose in most unbecoming positions to be photographed.'

In December 1930, the Fairfield Council in Sydney asked local police to take action against bathers using the picnic areas along the Georges River, after complaints from a local church representative regarding 'persons whose clothing verged on the indecent'.

It was a time when sun-worshipping was becoming a fad, especially among young people. As an early example of niche marketing, Country Life cork-tipped cigarettes promoted themselves as the 'firm favourite of Sydney's stalwart sun bakers'. The illustration shows a slim young flapper wearing a swimsuit with extremely large arm holes.

The first advertisements for body hair removal also appeared. One for X-Bazin, the 'Famous French way of Removing Hair', featured a 'clean limbed beach beauty' riding an aquaplane while proudly displaying her exposed and denuded armpit.

'You will see them at all the beaches this summer', warned the advertisement. 'Attractive girls with arms, limbs and underarms free from disfiguring hair.'

The 1930s witnessed a fad for the backless swimsuit, as much a cause of controversy then as the topless swimsuits would be in the future. Again, the moral police stepped in. The Reverend Cox, a Congregational Minister, said that such costumes affected the essential modesty of the pure woman. Backless women, he reflected, were not the kind to uplift the moral tone of the community.

The fad was most memorably celebrated by the poet Kenneth Slessor who was then writing topical verse for *Smith's Weekly*, a popular Sydney news magazine.

In 'Backless Betty from Bondi', Slessor celebrated the latest beach fashion, declaiming members of local council and other wowsers who were threatening to ban them.

'You aldermen who thunder out
Damnation for the Backless,
Your waists, no doubt, are rather stout,
Which makes you somewhat tactless;'

By the mid 1930s it appeared the shrinking swimsuit was about to disappear altogether. A mere 30 years after William Gocher dared to take Australia's first daylight swim, the virtues of nudity were being keenly debated in the letters section of *Health and Physical Culture* magazine, an Australian publication covering matters of fitness and wellbeing.

Nudism (illustrated by a few tasteful photos, some sent in by adventurous and mostly male readers) fitted in with this general theme and no doubt helped boost the magazine's circulation.

'Dear Sir', writes 'Atlantis' in a letter published in the September 1935 issue. 'It is very interesting to see your readers wrangling for and against the nude cult, and I'll bet some of them have never been in the nude in their lives. I am a semi-nudist and that is as far as any sane man or woman need go. As for mixed nudism—well, whoever started that idea needs a medical examination.'

The next struggle was for men to remove their tops.

When the Hawaiian swimmer and surfer Duke Kahanamoku visited Australia in 1915, becoming the first man to demonstrate the art of surfing while standing up, he was shown on posters riding a wave with his torso exposed. This was not allowed under Australia's strict bathing laws so he had to wear a singlet top in order to demonstrate his surfing skills.

This situation still applied in the 1930s when a Mr Jennings, a Member of the House of Representatives, declared that Glenelg Beach in Adelaide led the nation for daring bathing attire. The Mayor

The Duke was promoted as surfing bare to the waist, but had to put on a singlet when he toured Australian beaches.

of Glenelg, Mr W. Fisk, briskly defended the morals of his populace, suggesting that Jennings should have his eyes tested. 'Certainly we are not mollycoddles at Glenelg', he said, 'and we do not wish to interfere one iota with manufacturers of beautiful bathing costumes so long as those costumes are modest'.

Men's 10/6
"Ring-Back" Costumes for **7/11**

We're in for a torrid summer—have you your Costume yet? Here's the latest for men. "Ring-back" style in all-wool elastic rib knit, in shades of maroon, royal, black and seagull-grey. Sizes 34 to 40 inch chests.

A modest costume, according to Fisk, was one preventing the exposure of any of those parts of the body which, in general opinion, it was immodest to expose. That included a man's nipples. He emphasised that men were not allowed to roll their costumes down to the waist or wear trunks on his section of beach.

In New South Wales, the regulation against men swimming or sunbathing without a top (Local Government Ordinance No. 52, first introduced in 1907 when the neck to knee compromise was introduced) became a big issue in 1936 when Eric Spooner, the then Minister for Local Government, became its chief enforcer. By this stage it was customary for Sydney men to roll down the tops of their costumes while sitting on the beach. Spooner would put a stop to that.

Volunteer lifesavers who acted as beach inspectors reported few if any complaints from the public yet councils still felt compelled to enforce Ordinance 52, which became known nationally as The Spooner Ban. In November 1936 a personal protest was made by Alec Parkins, a member of the Manly Life Saving Club, who walked along his local beach wearing only a pair of shorts, shoes and socks. His nipples were exposed to the sun.

*And Mister Spooner takes a bath!*

Spooner was mercilessly sent up by the popular press.

*ERIC SYDNEY SPOONER—a Syd. Miller vision.*

Parkins had studied the regulations and noted the wording of one section: 'in any case where an inspector is of opinion that any person's bathing costume is indecent or inadequate ...' He suggested that by wearing shoes and socks he was not in a bathing costume and couldn't be prosecuted.

Beneath a photo of Parkins being escorted off the sand, the *Daily Telegraph* newspaper explained: 'His aim was to test the Spooner regulations. Is he in bathing costume if he wears shoes and socks?'

The honorary solicitor of the Surf Life Saving Association agreed to defend Parkins if the council decided to proceed against his client. His interpretation was that, according to the regulations, the indecency was not in uncovering your chest on the beach but in uncovering your chest to bathe. 'A law in which such contradictions are possible is obviously no law for a reputedly sane community', concluded the newspaper.

This was now a big issue. A few days later *The Sun* newspaper asked another legal expert, Mr W. J. Bradley, KC, what would happen if 20 000 or more men appeared on the beach at Bondi or Manly wearing only trunks. This now appeared likely.

'Each would be guilty of a breach of the law and would be liable to prosecution', he replied before adding that, 'the law-making authority, Parliament, is expected to recognize what we call public opinion, but if 90 per cent of the people in the community were in arms against a promulgated law, then, generally, we would expect Parliament to alter that law. If there were a genuine demonstration of protest, and then more protest, I think a position would be created which Parliament would have to consider—it would mean that a law was being kept on the statute books which was not wanted by the community.'

An initial act of protest came from the three honorary beach inspectors at Avalon on Sydney's northern peninsula, who resigned rather than act as 'amateur policemen'.

There were also resignations at Dee Why Beach where one rebel inspector, L. S. McDonald from Freshwater, said: 'If the clubs take this lying down they deserve what they get. They have the whole situation in their hands and can effectively show Mr Spooner their feelings. I would be one of the first to wear trunks in an organised protest.' Other inspectors said they would retain their positions but would refuse to arrest men without tops, as they had been refusing to do for several summers prior.

Even advertisers got in on the debate. 'We're in for a torrid summer—have you got your costume yet?' asked one department store, promoting their discounted Ring Back costumes in shades of maroon, royal, black and seagull grey. These were a compromise costume, allowing the wearer to be legally covered in front yet still get an almost complete tan on the back and shoulders.

What happened in the summer of 1936 was a stalemate. Many male bathers rolled down their tops in defiance of the regulation and most beach inspectors refused to charge them. Equally defiant was Eric Spooner who, in May 1937, said he didn't intend to modify the regulations in spite of public protest and pressure by bathing costume manufacturers, claiming it was up to the councils to enforce the law or not.

'This is odd', remarked *Smith's Weekly* in 1939. 'For although the NSW Cabinet contains several full-grown, pure-bred specimens of the genus wowser, amiable, chain-smoking Eric Spooner is not one of them. Personally he did not care a hoot about banning trunks', they added, suggesting that his motives were purely pragmatic. The implication was that he only defended the ordinance to appease some of the more conservative local councils.

In retrospect, it was an unwise decision. Spooner held ambitions to be Premier of NSW but lost out in a party room challenge. While he had an otherwise distinguished career in both State and Federal Parliament (where he served briefly as Minister for War Organisation of Industry in the Menzies Government) he remains chiefly remembered as a figure of fun, lampooned mercilessly by cartoonists. To be painted a wowser is a political kiss of death. It was a lesson in political reality that aspiring premier Neville Wran would be careful to learn in 40 years time when he shrewdly supported the introduction of nude beaches in New South Wales.

Absurd or not, the Spooner Ban was one in a continuing series of battles over beach attire that have spiced up the sands over a century. There had been protests over men's bathing skirts in 1907 and there would come a day when women would also be demanding the right to remove their tops.

# chapter **six**

# Mr Bandparts

Norman Lindsay is one of the elite to have been banned for both the drawn image and the written word. In 1913 his first novel, *A Curate in Bohemia*, could only be published after he had reworked his cover illustration, covering the model's exposed breast with a kimono.

Memories of his childhood in Creswick were first recorded in his novel *Redheap*, which he had begun writing in his spare time as early as 1908. After sitting on a shelf for a few decades, the manuscript was finally published in 1930 in Britain by Faber & Faber. It remained banned in Australia until December 1959.

In this largely autobiographical work (Redheap is his

The cover of Lindsay's novel *A Curate in Bohemia* had to be modified to satisfy the censors.

fictional name for Creswick and the protagonist, Robert Piper, is clearly a facsimile of the young Norman Lindsay), there are several sexual scenes that were considered shocking for the time, including Robert's fumbling seduction of a servant girl.

'Experimentally he unbuttoned her blouse, but the intrusion on its privacies was not resisted. Still, inspiration was begotten by the tender caress of her breasts. He began to kiss her, and a responsive shiver enlightened him. This pacific pose was her admission of desire, the mute offering of her body to love. Disturbed and charmed, Robert possessed her. It was a jumbled, unarranged consummation, but it was divine.'

This was hot stuff for the day, yet the bulk of Australian complaints had more to do with Lindsay picking on a small town. 'Why', asked the *Sydney Morning Herald*, 'has Lindsay turned on a little place near Ballarat?'

The first few pages begin with Robert having an erotic fantasy during a Sunday service. This was, as Lindsay writes, 'a diversion he frequently employed to mitigate the boredom of church'. The object of sacrilegious lust on this occasion is the parson's daughter, 'young and plump'—just how Norman liked his women.

It's easy to imagine Lindsay laughing out loud as he bashed out another wicked episode on his trusty Remington in his cluttered studio in the Blue Mountains. Lindsay surely knew what reaction this book would

'Is Norman Lindsay a genius?', asked the *Sydney Mail* in 1918.

draw unless, as he suggests in his autobiography, he wrote it purely as a diversion without ever expecting it to be published. As if to bait his detractors further, one of the main characters is called Mr Bandparts.

When it was published in England, *Redheap* was seen as a damning but hilarious reflection on Australian small-town life.

'What sort of a dog-box is it for a man to spend his life in?' he asks via Robert Piper.

Such questions were not to be asked in 1930 and, as soon as it was announced that the English edition was about to be sold in Australia, things started to happen. One story is that Norman Lindsay's own mother, Mary, then 82 and still resident in Creswick, wrote to the Department of Customs suggesting that her son's book was libelous and should not be allowed into Australia.

After scathing reviews in, among others, the Melbourne *Argus*—'through the mouth of a particularly nasty adolescent and a tedious inebriate are expressed a number of opinions upon life which are neither new or true'—a Mr Horace Richardson appealed in the Victorian State Parliament for the banning of the book by the Federal Government. Richardson would have been especially offended as he was a leading member of the Baptist Church.

The member for Bendigo, the federal seat in which Creswick sits, then took up the campaign in the House of Representatives. Mr F. M. Forde, the Acting Minister for Customs, ordered that advance copies be sent from England, a process which took several weeks. By 21 May 1930, he and several other prominent officers had read the book and Mr Forde announced that *Redheap* was to be prohibited on the grounds that it contained passages that were indecent or obscene.

The 16 000 copies which were then on a ship from England were intercepted on arrival and sent back whence they came.

One reason why the Vice Squad seized the December 1930 issue of *Art in Australia*.

By this stage Lindsay, a battle-scarred veteran of censorship, knew exactly how to respond. *Smith's Weekly*, no friend of wowserdom, shrewdly invited Lindsay to comment on the Customs decision and gave him a full page to vent his anger.

Next to unflattering illustrations of Mr Forde, Norman Lindsay wrote: 'Silly devils! They can no more censor *Redheap* than they can censor the atmosphere. All they can do is make temporary nuisances of themselves, and cause Australian booksellers to lose a little present profit. A fine spectacle they present, making a noise like an egg, censoring a book that has already sold out its first edition in England!'

After more of the same he closed with a personal message to the Acting Minister.

'As for you, Mr Forde, pass—for the present. But, oh, what a perfect ass you are.'

Later that year, a special Norman Lindsay issue of *Art in Australia* was released and sold well. Perhaps it's only coincidence but in June 1931 a squad of police arrived at the publishers' offices and seized everything they could find to do with the Norman Lindsay edition, including printers' blocks and stereotypes and unsold copies. During the raid one of the sergeants was heard to say, 'I've read what this man has had to say about the police force.'

The officer was probably referring to a comment made by Lindsay concerning the banning of *Redheap*. The quote now seemed doubly ironic.

> 'The only thing disclosed to me ... is the astonished discovery that Australian officialdom is still the pure product of the convict system. A policeman's baton to settle all questions. The departments confer. Quite arbitrary—one medieval baron to another. There is something extremely disgusting in having one's work pawed by a policeman.'

The publishers, Sydney Ure Smith and Leon Gellert, were charged with 'having caused to be issued an obscene publication'. For a while Norman Lindsay also feared that his studio would be raided, possibly by policemen wielding batons, and he would also be charged. While in Sydney to discuss the prosecution, he noticed a *Smith's Weekly* poster outside a newsagency. It read: 'Will Norman Lindsay Be Arrested?'

He wasn't. The case was dismissed.

The *Cautious Amorist* was another Norman Lindsay best-seller, first published in America, then by T. Werner Laurie Ltd in London. It was almost to be expected that a shipment of the British edition was seized by Australian Customs officers. 'Norman hardly bothered to discuss the ban even with friends', writes John Hetherington 'he was becoming used to the ways of Australian censors'.

The book is a story of three men and one woman stranded on a desert island. Among other highlights it contains perhaps the first detailed description of foot fetishism in Australian literature, when Gibble the clergyman overhears the following conversation between Pat, an Irish stoker, and Sadie, the mandatory voluptuous siren. Pat begins the dialogue.

'If you will not put your foot on me, will you lend me one of your shoes?'

'What for?'

'It's a fancy I have to be holdin' something your feet have trod in.'

'You're a fool.'

'I am. An' a fool I wish to be. Sittin' here lookin' at you. Will you sit quiet a minute while I kiss your feet?'

The Reverend Gibble, himself displaying signs of overt voyeurism, then struggles to see what is happening.

'In a frenzy of haste and silence he squirmed in among the bushes until he was able to overlook a section of the rock pool with Sadie perched on a rock, sedately plaiting her hair … by another exercise of squirming he was able to discover Pat stretched at her feet, embracing them.'

Typically, Norman Lindsay describes this act of fetishism as both normal and mutual.

'Possibly Sadie's calmness was the most confounding aspect of this sylvan tableau' he writes. 'She went on doing her hair without haste and without any concern for the prostrate orientalist at her feet.'

Lindsay's seventh novel, *Age of Consent*, was first published in New York by Farrar & Rinehart in 1938. Needless to say it was banned in Australia until 1962. Six years later it was made into a film starring English actors James Mason and Helen Mirren.

Originally set on the South Coast of New South Wales (changed to a Great Barrier Reef island for the film), this is the story of the disillusioned painter Bradly Mudgett who arrives seeking inspiration. He convinces a local girl, Cora, to pose for him and then seduces her. This is Lolita with an Australian accent. Mudgett is 40 and there's a suspicion that Cora is, as the title suggests, a year or so underage.

In the book the inevitable seduction is merely hinted at, but in the 1968 film it could be more graphically depicted. Even without this sexual act the book would have been banned, among other reasons, for its direct references to then unspoken parts of the female anatomy. Let's cross briefly to Cora posing for Mudgett in a sunlit lagoon, where the artist,

ABOVE and NEXT PAGE: Helen Mirren made an ideal Cora in the 1968 film of Lindsay's *Age of Consent.*

searching for the right amount of skin tone, asks his model to show more of her legs.

'With one of her strenuous wriggles, which either confessed embarrassment, or rejected it, she pulled the skirt up, but it was so short that being pulled up, it came above her thighs, and revealed their warm mystery golden with light reflected from the water.'

And so appears perhaps the first description of a woman's pubic region in Australian literature. To complete the picture (one which Australians were not allowed to enjoy for another 24 years), Lindsay included a black and white illustration of this scene, one which remains one of the most erotic ever drawn.

As if predicting the response of the wowsers, Lindsay writes, 'it was a bit too daring, that pose; buyers mightn't like it'.

Later Mudgett convinces Cora to remove her dress entirely while posing on the beach, which inspires another illustration and some more of Lindsay's purple prose.

'Bradly was instantly charmed by the sweet revealing of her honey-tinted nudity: the smooth plumpness of a youthful body just arrived at a mature feminine canon.'

This may be a typical Norman Lindsay fantasy, yet he wants to show that Cora is a willing participant—'those interludes established her right to the freedom of a naked body forever', he suggests. 'She was mysteriously happy, as if her skimpy frock had been a weight on the spiritual release of her nudity.' Later there is also the implication that she is the willing participant in her own seduction.

In 1938 it was radical thought to even suggest that women might actually enjoy being looked at while naked and might enjoy having sex. Lindsay's book still had the power to shock in 1968 when the film version was released.

The movie was an English production, with English actor James Mason speaking with an unconvincing ocker accent. The teenage Helen Mirren as Cora is much more agreeable casting, and in the essential nude scenes lives

Cora as seen by Norman Lindsay.

NORMAN LINDSAY COPYRIGHT H. A. & C. GLAD

up to Norman Lindsay's written instructions for 'the smooth plumpness of a youthful body'.

Equally erotic are some underwater scenes in which the Australian model and scuba diving champion Cathy Troutt filled in as the body double for Mirren. The film seems to have passed through the censors without any serious snipping and can be seen as an indication of a more permissive society.

Lindsay died before he could see *Sirens*, the best-known Norman Lindsay film, loosely based on his life. It's possible he might have enjoyed it but, preferring his woman a bit meatier than Elle Macpherson, I doubt it. 'I've got no use for these starved hawks', he famously said. Given his literary and artistic content, it's reasonable to assume that Norman Lindsay himself lived a life of debauchery. The truth appears to be the opposite. In his biography of Lindsay, the poet Douglas Stewart records that his close friend was 'very moderate and normal, and that he seemed to live in a state of chastity all the years I had known him'.

Lindsay's primary passion was for work. In their early period at Springwood, Rose Lindsay liked to throw lavish, bohemian parties but while these raged on into the night Norman Lindsay took refuge in his studio, oblivious to the fact that real life revelries, if not orgies, were taking place around him.

Douglas Stewart describes one of these Springwood parties, as related by Lindsay himself … 'one highly respectable married lady of my acquaintance tells a prettier story of how embarrassed she was one night in her youth to find herself tripping naked through the moonlit cypresses and angophoras to bathe in the swimming pool; while, around her, various prominent citizens of Sydney, whom I forbear to name, gamboled like playful goats'.

Lindsay stressed that this was only hearsay. He wasn't there, gamboling like a goat. He was busy at work in his studio.

# chapter **seven**

# Inversion and perversion

**A**rthur Phillip, the first Governor of New South Wales, once said that murderers and sodomites deserved to be thrown to the cannibals. Approximately 200 years later, the first Gay and Lesbian Mardi Gras took place down the main street of Kings Cross in 1978, not far from where Phillip had landed. On that day the Kings Cross police made 58 arrests and bashed gay activists.

'Strange Life; Serious Allegations'—shocked Australians first learnt of Sydney's homosexual underworld.

In between these events, homosexuality was treated as both a criminal act and, in some instances, an act of insanity.

One of the first public homosexual scandals was reported by Sydney's notorious *Truth* newspaper on 22 November 1936 when, with undisguised delight, they covered the scandalous details of the divorce court proceedings of George Bellingham Roberts and his wife Isabelle.

George Roberts, former secretary to the Earl of Beauchamp in London, was described as a 'sartorially resplendent man-about-town'. His wife, formerly Miss Belle Finlayson, was a Sydney society beauty. After their marriage in 1933 the couple lived initially at Carthona, a mansion at Darling Point. They were regularly featured in the social pages.

The underlying reason for their separation was hinted at in the *Truth*'s sub-heading, 'Bride Thrown into Queer World'. In seeking a divorce after three years of marriage, she invoked grounds 'seldom if ever used by a wife against a husband'. Or, as the *Truth* put it as plainly as they dared, 'allegations were made that concerned men'. These men were referred to in court as A, B and C.

This was the synopsis according to the *Truth*'s court reporter.

'She fell in love with Roberts, and married him. But little did she know then of the life that she was to face in the coming years—a life that was one day to end her romance and bring her to court to tell of a man who burned her finger and forehead with a lighted cigarette, who sat in bed with a shawl over his shoulders, while another man, with apron on, served him with breakfast; of a man who locked her up and tied her hand and foot so she could not go to church.'

Mr Jack Shand appeared for Mrs Roberts.

'In this case', he told the all-male jury, 'it is my duty on behalf of my client to put before you facts which are extremely grave and extremely unpleasant. But, however difficult it may be for this young lady to go into the box to depose of these facts, I am going to ask for your sympathy, and you will see that no more unpleasant matter could be possible for a young woman to endure, a lady gently nurtured, to have to bring before a court of law in which there are large numbers of the public.'

Shand quickly got to the core of the case.

'This man, handsome in face and figure, was a man to whom the decent and natural conduct of married life meant not only nothing, but less than nothing … He was a man steeped in every type of abnormal conduct.' A pause for dramatic effect. 'It is my duty to put before you all the intimate circumstances of their married life.'

And so Sydney, or that proportion which subscribed to the *Truth*, heard the intimate details of a man who, from the first night of their marriage, occupied a separate bed in a separate room.

'And then', explained Mr Shand, 'he began to invite there certain men friends of his, who showed quite clearly later what type of men they were.' And then, 'he began flaunting the unnatural and indecent before her. You will probably have little doubt that there was something in his mind, the desire to make his conduct so impossible, so disgusting that he would be free of her, and free to associate with those unnatural persons with whom he surrounded himself. During this time he called her disgusting names. He advised her to take a lover and said that life would be very dull for her.

He used to put on the dressing table indecent pictures of a boy and a man. There were several of these and she used to tear them up.'

Later, as Shand told the jury and hence the rest of Australia, there were also live demonstrations of indecency.

'One man he brought there, and in front of his wife and this man, despite their protests, he went about naked, and this other man, to use his own words, "admired Roberts' beautiful body". And said she ought to be proud to have such man as her husband. She heard things that caused her to fly from their presence. They used a queer jargon that the ordinary man does not hear of. They used to address each other in a distinctly feminine way.'

'I am not going to elaborate on it', concluded Shand, 'but this was a strange world to which this young lady was introduced.'

Then, elaborating on it, he revealed that George Roberts had forced her to read passages from books that are 'fortunately censored in this country ... one a book written by a most abnormal man, D. H. Lawrence.' The book was *Lady Chatterley's Lover*, a prohibited import. At which point Shand handed the jury an extract from this banned book.

After they had absorbed the indecent writing of that 'most abnormal man', Shand continued. 'Gentlemen, from that you will get an idea of the type of man he [Roberts] turned out to be, a man guilty of every sort of inversion and perversion one could imagine. Added to this also was a sadistic temperament of which apparently he was proud.'

Thus, Shand insinuated that the reading of D. H. Lawrence was a sure-fire indication of perversion.

# chapter **eight**

# **Boult-upright**

**W**hat would become Australia's strangest obscenity trial began ordinarily enough with a knock on the door of Room 83, a rented space on the second floor of the Brookman Buildings in Grenfell Street, Adelaide. From here Maxwell Harris, a young man with literary pretensions, published a magazine he called *Angry Penguins*.

Sometime in the afternoon of 1 August 1944, Harris was paid a visit by a man called Jacobus Vogelesang (sometimes spelt Vogelsang) brandishing a copy of the Autumn edition. It featured a Sidney Nolan illustration, *The Sole Arabian Tree*, on

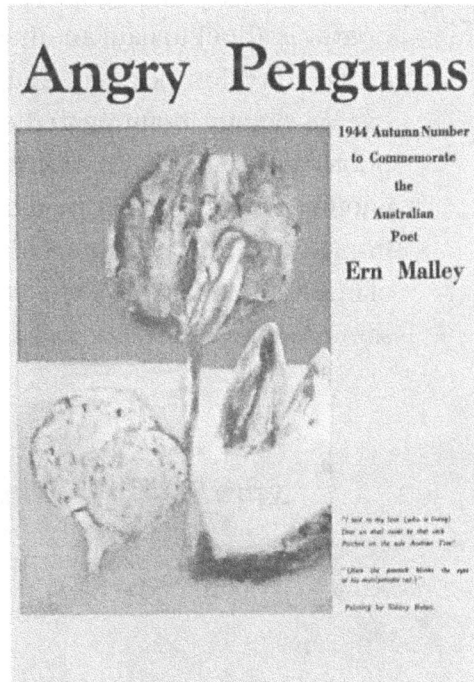

The offending issue of *Angry Penguins*, with cover art by Sidney Nolan.

the cover. If Harris knew his Dutch he would have known that Vogelesang's name translates into 'birdsong', but the stern man of that name was not there for pleasantries. Vogelesang was a policeman and he was on official duty. 'Are you acquainted with all the poems in the Ern Malley section?' he asked. Harris said he was; an understatement of grand proportions. It had already been established, to Harris' great embarrassment, that Ern Malley was the fictional creation of James McAuley and Harold Stewart, two poets who wrote what was later described as 'consciously and deliberately concocted nonsense' in order to ridicule the avant-garde style championed by *Angry Penguins*. They pulled off one of Australia's great literary hoaxes by claiming, via Ern's equally ficti-tious sister Ethel, that these poems had been found in her late brother's bedroom. Now, courtesy of a man called Birdsong, the hoax was about to gain another, even more surreal dimension.

'Do you think the poem is suggestive of indecency?' asked Detec-tive Vogelesang, pointing to the Ern Malley poem 'Boult to Marina' published on page 11. Harris, no doubt wondering if this was another hoax, said that he didn't. The detective quoted two lines from the poem: 'Part of me remains, wench, Boult-upright / The rest of me drops off into the night' before asking again, 'Do you think that some people could place an indecent interpretation on it?'

Tormented poet. Max Harris in 1945.

Vogelesang could, and he intended to do something about it.

After seeking legal advice Max Harris started to take the matter seriously. He had written a novel *The Vegetative Eye*, also in the modernist style. All unsold copies of that book were secretly transferred from his rooms to the nearby bureau of the *Australian Women's Weekly* where an accomplice hid them under back copies of that most wholesome of magazines. This, he figured, was the last place anyone would look.

The *Angry Penguins* trial began on 5 September 1944 in the Adelaide Police Court. It was the first time that Australian poetry had ever been under threat of censorship and, as Michael Heyward notes in his book *The Ern Malley Affair*, this was 'the hottest show in town … the courtroom on Victoria Square was "crowded as a picture theatre", and buzzing with anticipation'.

D. C. Williams of the Crown Solicitor's Department headed the prosecution case. Another talented Adelaide lawyer, Eric Millhouse, was appointed to defend Harris who was charged under Section 108 of the South Australian Police Act—an ancient law relating to 'indecent advertisements' (further defined as 'printed matter of an indecent immoral or obscene nature'). The act had been on the books since 1897 when the test of indecency was specified as 'whether the tendency of the matter charged as obscenity is to deprave and corrupt those whose minds are open to such immoral influences, and into whose hands a publication of this sort may fall'.

Harris was by now a very angry penguin. Under this law, literary or artistic merit could not be used as a defence, nor was the fact that the Ern Malley poems were a hoax of any relevance. By this stage 13 passages in the magazine had been identified as possibly offensive. Only seven were in the works of Ern Malley, the others were by bona fide writers, including Harris himself.

Perhaps more daunting to Harris was his growing premonition that the trial was a moral vendetta set up by Adelaide's powerful group of Catholic conservatives. From the beginning he felt that this was a battle he couldn't win.

His sense of doom deepened when, as he had previously in Room 83, Detective Vogelesang appeared in the capacity of freelance literary critic. He was the sole crown witness.

> 'The genitals refer to the sexual parts', Vogelesang observed on one occasion. 'I think it is unusual for the sexual parts to be referred to in poetry.'

Genitalia also features in another Ern Malley poem, 'The Journey North', a slab of which the detective felt inspired to recite in front of the courtroom. This was one of the more surreal moments in literary history.

> 'New Year brought its concertinas in,
> the redundant festivities of piano and song
> for the flatchested women of the camp,
> whose genitals ached like very hell
> for the passionate copulation in satin
> and passivity by the lowtuned radio,
> waking to the morning aubade of trams.'

Regardless of McAuley and Stewart's admission that the poems were intended purely as parody of the modernist style, the literary detective placed his own interpretation on the quoted work. 'Does it mean that the woman's sexual parts are aching for an evening dress?' he pondered.

Harris seemed to agree with this suggestion.

Vogelesang responded. 'Don't you think that is immoral?'

And so the trial continued, as if scripted by Monty Python himself. Under cross-examination, Vogelesang was asked why he felt the expression 'Boult-upright'—the one he first raised, so to speak, in Max Harris' office—was so offensive.

'I don't think it could mean that Boult was an upright man', he said. 'It offends my decency to suggest that a character means that he wants sexual intercourse. I think that is immoral. That governs my opinion with regard to all these matters, where intercourse is referred to, I take it as immoral, in the circumstances in which we find them here. I would consider under certain circumstances that it was indecent to talk about the sexual act, to discuss it with a friend, for example.'

Another poem that Vogelesang found indecent was 'Night Piece'.

'I think there is a suggestion of indecency about it', he told the court, before explaining why. 'Apparently, someone is shining a torch in the dark … I have found that people who go into parks at night go there for immoral purposes …'

He also found the word 'incestuous' offensive, although he admitted he didn't known what the word meant, especially in context. The offending word appears in the final two lines of 'Egyptian Register': 'On the mausoleum of my incestuous/ And self-fructifying death.'

A pause for thought. 'I think there is a suggestion of indecency about it', he said.

The prosecution rested its case. The court was adjourned until 26 September so that the defence would have time to prepare its case. Max Harris felt slightly more positive about the outcome, even if he and his wife were abused by strangers as they walked down the street … 'the notoriety is distracting me so that I'm having to pull myself together all the time', he wrote to his friend and co-editor, John Reed. 'I'm taking too much Nembutal for the sake of sleep.'

The insomnia may have deepened when Harris learned that Millhouse was unable to continue because of prior engagements.

A lesser legal talent was called in as an ill-prepared replacement. In the end the defence collapsed under the weight of its own gravitas. Text was laboriously dissected line by line in an effort to trace its literary influence and therefore importance. There followed a marathon two-day effort by Harris, meticulously analysing works that, in the case of Ern Malley, were written as nonsense.

> 'Harris had spent the entire day in the box, and seemed to be ahead on points, even if some of his interpretations of the poetry were not altogether convincing' writes Michael Heyward. 'But the cross-examination had one unforeseen result: it conjured Ern Malley into renewed existence.'

As it turned out the defence had erred in deciding to treat Ern Malley seriously in the first place. It was a point fully exploited by the prosecution.

> 'The man in the street, hearing the term "unforgivable rape" (as used in Ern Malley's poem "Sweet William") don't you think he would take it as having sexual connotation?' Williams asked of Max Harris.

'I don't know what the ordinary man in the street thinks', Harris replied. Williams had been hoping he'd say that.

> 'You consider yourself above the ordinary man in the street, don't you?'

The question was withdrawn and rephrased but things were going exactly as Harris had originally feared. He, and not the magazine, was on trial here. Williams said as much in his summing-up when he suggested that the Malley poems had been deliberately used for the purpose of referring to sex: 'the approach of Harris to this sort of rubbish, a man who said that minds have to be attuned to higher things, is shown by the fact that he could not tell me the meaning of one of the words he was questioned about.'

After judgement was reserved, Harris sent off a terse but prophetic telegram to John Reed.

'DEFENCE WEAK WILLIAMS VICIOUS OUTLOOK BLACK.'

On Friday 20 October, Stipendiary Magistrate L. C. Clarke delivered his 20-page judgement. He began optimistically enough by declaring that 'the public is so used to somewhat gross literary aphrodisiacs that a work must be rather more daring than could have been published fifty years ago in order to unbalance the susceptible.'

The magistrate then turned his attention to the 13 passages in question and, as Vogelesang had done back in August, his thoughts quickly turned to the words 'Boult-upright' … 'obviously a very poor pun', he decided. 'He (the mythical Ern Malley, one suspects) is referring to this purpose of having sexual intercourse with her'.

He was less sure of the meaning of the next line—'the rest of me drops off into the night'—but said he had no doubt at all in finding that the first stanza was indecent.

By this stage Harris knew that he was done. In closing, Clarke found none of the passages obscene or immoral but did find that some were 'indecent advertisements', a lesser crime according to his interpretation of Section 108. In the manner of the stern schoolmaster reprimanding the smutty little schoolboy, Clarke warned the accused that he displayed 'far too great a fondness for sexual references'.

Max Harris was fined five pounds in lieu of six weeks' imprisonment.

Outside the court he appeared defiant, suggesting to reporters that he would appeal and, in any case, would continue to publish

*Angry Penguins*, even if it was not available in his puritanical home state. The conviction, wrist-slapping as it was, was nevertheless condemned by other artists and civil libertarians. The *Argus* in Melbourne published a protest letter although the two hoaxers (then in military service and based at the Victoria Barracks in Melbourne) were conspicuous by their silence. Stewart and McAuley later claimed they had composed a letter to the *Adelaide Advertiser* in which they declaimed the verdict and suggested that they, if anyone, should have been the ones on trial. They must have thought better of this suggestion and this letter was never sent.

In the end Max Harris decided not to appeal, in part because legal advice offered him little hope of success, in part because the climactic events of the Second World War made a legal battle over the meaning of 'Boult-upright' suddenly seem less important.

He moved to Melbourne in 1945 and, as threatened, continued to publish his magazine without distribution in South Australia. But only three more *Angry Penguins* were produced before Harris moved on to other projects. Later in life Harris returned to Adelaide and wrote a chatty column for a Sunday tabloid newspaper. In this more prosaic role, he was noted for his vitriolic attacks on what passed for the Establishment in the Athens of the South.

Perhaps he had a right to be bitter. If, as some claim, censorship is more about the established powers retaining control than about actual content, Harris could fairly say that he had been the victim of a pack-rape by Adelaide conservatives.

In his own epitaph to this strange little chapter in history, Michael Heyward notes that shortly after the trial, Detective Vogelesang was given a special mention by the South Australian Commissioner of Police for his 'zealousness and competency in securing evidence for the prosecution of an indecent publication'.

It was a peak period for the banning of books. In 1939, close to 5000 books were on Australia's prohibited list, including such classics as Ernest Hemingway's *A Farewell to Arms*, Aldous Huxley's

*Brave New World*, George Orwell's *Down and Out in Paris and London* and Daniel Defoe's *Moll Flanders*. James Joyce's *Ulysses*, first banned in 1929, was released in 1937 when, after pressure from a church organisation, it was prohibited again in 1941. Sir Frederick Stewart, Minister for External Affairs, described it as a 'collection of unadulterated fifth'. A Mr Lawrence of the New South Wales Legislative Assembly said he would change his name if ever D. H. Lawrence's banned book, *Lady Chatterley's Lover*, was made available in Australia.

Most banned books were English or European (with the notable exception of the thrice-banned Norman Lindsay) but shortly after the war two Australian works were added to the list.

In 1946 Lawson Glassop's book, *We Were the Rats*, was declared obscene in Sydney Central Summons Court. This war-time novel, set during the siege of Tobruk, was first published in 1944. Dialogue reminiscent of the Ern Malley trial occurred in this case when, during cross-examination, Mr Dovey checked the literary credentials of the Vice Squad sergeant who had instigated the charge.

Dovey: Have you ever heard of Byron?
Sergeant: No.
Dovey: He was a Lord.
Sergeant: Yes, I've heard of him.
Dovey: Do you know if he was on Lord Mountbatten's staff?
Sergeant: I don't know.
Dovey: Do you know if he was a writer?
Sergeant: I don't know.
Dovey: Do you know if he was a war correspondent?
Sergeant: I don't know.
Dovey: Have you heard of Shelley?
Sergeant: I know a man named Shelley but I take it you refer to an author or something. I have never heard of the name Shelley as a man who wrote something.

'Obscene', said the Sydney Central Summons Court.

The magistrate decided that *We Were the Rats* was obscene and the publishers, Angus & Robertson, were fined ten pounds. Even though the RSL defended the merits of the book, it remained on the banned list until 1965.

A more extraordinary case was that of Robert S. Close's 1945 book, *Love Me Sailor*—a novel about the adventures of a nymphomaniac. Close and his publishers, Georgian House, faced the Melbourne Criminal Court on charges of having published a book containing obscene matter.

'The morals of a community, especially the youth of the community, are to be safeguarded', said Mr Justice Martin in passing sentence. 'I regard your book as a gross assault on that morality.'

The publishers were fined 500 pounds. Robert S. Close was fined 100 pounds and sentenced to three months imprisonment. He was led from the court in handcuffs. After the severity of the sentence was questioned by civil libertarians, the Court of Criminal Appeal annulled the gaol sentence.

Close decided to live overseas and his banned book became a best-seller in Germany and France where it was promoted with the slogan 'the author of this book went to gaol' on the dust jacket.

Equally significant are the books that might have been banned during this period but weren't. In 1946 Ruth Park's book *The Harp in the South*, set in the slums of Surry Hills, was awarded first prize in the *Sydney Morning Herald*'s Novel Competition and was serialised in the newspaper in January 1947.

This publication attracted great controversy with a typical protest coming from the Willoughby Methodist Parsonage which, after discussing the prize-winners at their quarterly meeting, declared that 'the fact that the three leading prizes have been awarded to novels which deal

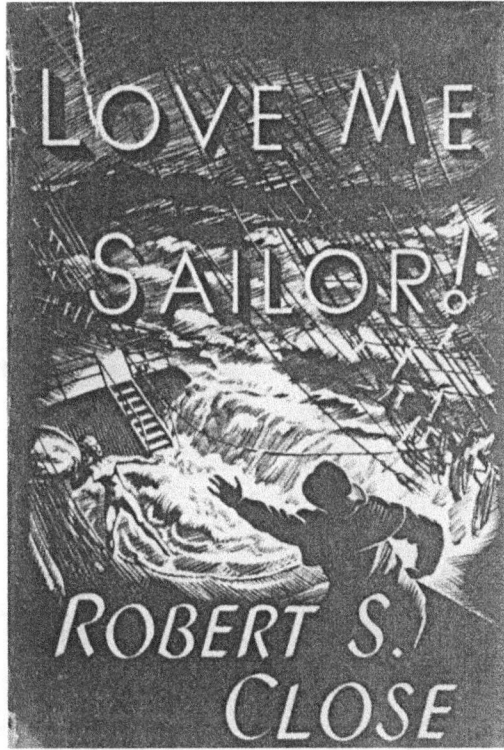

*Love Me Sailor* was another banned book. Robert Close was led from court in handcuffs.

so largely with the sordid side of life, as indicated in the synopses, is detrimental to the proper observance of moral standards'. The parsonage regretted their publication, as did Miss Margaret Anderson of nearby Killara who protested specifically against Ruth Park's book from her hospital bed.

'I am ill, recovering from an accident, but while there is breath left in my body I must protest against such an outrage against decency as is portrayed in the first chapter of the prize-winning novel' she wrote, later describing the work as 'unadulterated filth'.

# the Harp in the South

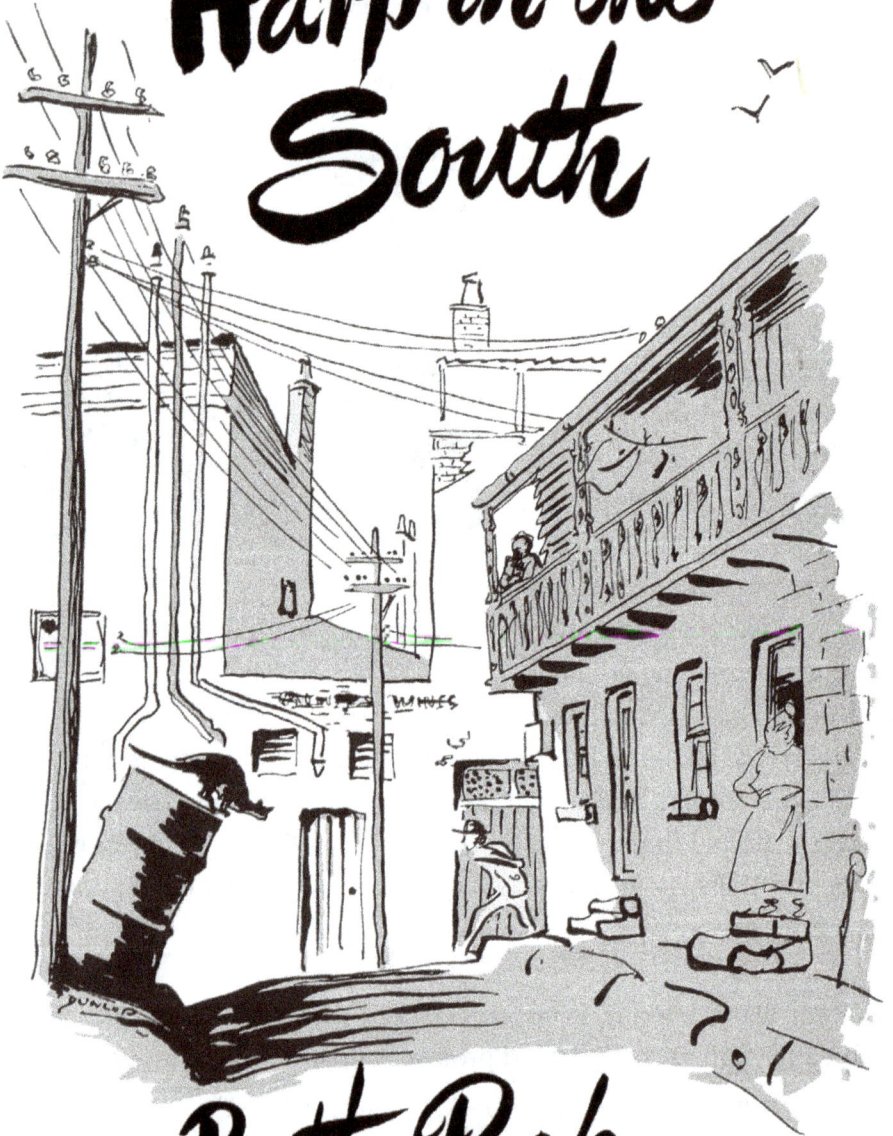

## Ruth Park

Also calling for a ban was 'Another Critic' from Croydon who complained about the 'easy and blasphemous use of the name of God, the thinly-veiled references to vulgar expressions, and the descriptions of the amorous conduct of a young couple in a park, make very sordid reading, and can do nothing but corrupt the minds of those who indulge in it. Must our literary talent dig into cesspits to produce mental food for the people?' he or she wondered. 'Where are our censors that such writings are allowed to become part of our literary possessions?'

In this case our censors might have been deterred from taking action because of the equal numbers of comments in praise of Park's novel. Prominent among these was one from no less than Warwick Fairfax, the eminent Managing Director of the *Sydney Morning Herald*. In the guise of editorial comment he supported the right of the modern novelist to seek inspiration in the slums of Surry Hills as much as in the Point Piper mansions he was used to.

Few first-time novelists had such influential support.

OPPOSITE: 'Unadulterated filth', declared one reader of Ruth Park's first novel.

# chapter nine
# Fun in little bohemia

In 1947 it was reported that Dame Enid Lyons, Australia's first female Member of the House of Representatives, wanted closer censorship of films imported from England. The mother of 11, and widow of former Prime Minister Joe Lyons, noted that all major American films had to first gain approval from the Catholic League of Decency. The same moral filter didn't apply in England and she was worried that these films permitted 'an unwelcome degree of frankness'.

She didn't mention Australian films, probably because so few were made. One of the few local productions to have troubled the censor so far over possible obscenity was *The Silence of Dean Maitland*, produced and

Charlotte Francis challenged the censors in *The Silence of Dean Maitland* in 1934.

directed by the esteemed Ken G. Hall in 1934. The subject matter was controversial enough, concerning a clergyman who denies that he is the father of his lover's child. The censor was also troubled by the appearance of American actress Charlotte Francis who emerges in one scene wearing only a small towel wrapped around her body. The towel struggles to hide what had to be concealed in that era.

After the censorship authorities demanded several cuts, Hall and his Cinesound Productions company decided to make this a public issue. The weight of opinion resulted in less savage cutting and, thanks to the publicity, his film had a good box office response.

It wasn't only major studio productions that got into trouble. When Sydney detectives raided the fun parlour at Manly Wharf in 1947, they were surprised to discover that a model featuring in three of the six confiscated movies was a Sydney girl, Moira Claux. She was then 16 years old.

One of the 16-millimetre films police seized from the arcade was a silent production called *Water Nymph*, playing on a What The Butler Saw machine. For a penny, viewers were able to see some shaky black and white footage of a naked Moira diving into a forest pool. Another machine featured a still photograph of Moira taken during the filming, while a third showed a studio portrait of her posing as Salome. Three other films taken during the raid were peep show productions imported

Moira Claux, the muse of Woolloomooloo.

from America. As with Charlotte Francis, these censored films would make Moira famous.

She was the Australian-born daughter of Kleber Claux, a gentle eccentric who ran a fruit stall in Liverpool Street outside the Central Courts. With his full beard and habit of wearing shorts and sandals even in the middle of winter, he resembled a figure from some previous century. This image was reinforced when he was cast as an extra in the film *Eureka Stockade*. He appears in the very first scene where he strikes the ground with a pickaxe and shouts 'Gold!'

Born in France, Kleber Claux had been a conscientious objector in the First World War and remained a pacifist and vegetarian all his life. Those who knew him soon learnt of his philosophy of free thought and love of nudism. He started the first nudist colony in Australia and his family had all grown up following the naturist lifestyle.

If not for the sensation of a local identity being on display, police might well have quietly fined the arcade manager Harold Spry a token amount, stored the films in a locker, then moved on to more serious matters. But the tabloid newspapers knew a good story when they stumbled upon one, and in interviews Moira delivered exactly what they wanted.

'I am opposed to the suggestive sex pictures which show models in postures and actions designed to arouse sexual emotion', she told *The Sun* reporter, 'but I believe natural nude studies are refreshing and artistic. I only pose for pictures which show nature as it is, and which may give some fillip to the healthy practice of nudism.'

Described as a 'striking brownette' in *The Sun*, Moira explained that she had felt much more uncomfortable posing for the Salome photograph, in which she appeared seductively draped in robes, than she had when posing nude for the cameras. Although she agreed with the banning of imported American films, she added, 'I cannot understand the censors objecting to any of the pictures in which I figure'.

By stating this in print, and agreeing to have her photo published, she became an instant celebrity. For the late 1940s this was radical thought indeed. Here she was, barely 16, eloquently enforcing her right to appear naked. In further interviews with the *Sunday Sun* (under the headline 'Nude Films All in a Day's Work') she revealed she had been working part-time as an artist's model since the age of 14, posing for life drawing classes at the East Sydney Technical College (now School of Arts) and the Bond Street Sketch Club.

Her parents fully approved and even her school friends at Dover Heights Home Science School seemed to accept her chosen method of earning pocket money. They gave her the nickname 'No Clo'.

In 1948 Julie Norman from *Woman* magazine wrote a lengthy and balanced feature story on the Claux family, then living in Botany, although she appears to have been mildly shocked by the appearance of nude photos of the family on top of the piano. Her article may have been the first to logically explain the theories of nudism to middle-class Australia. While a 78 rpm recording of 'St Louis Blues' played on the gramophone, Miss Norman sipped European-strength coffee while Moira, as usual, held court.

> 'There is nothing shameful or morally wrong in posing in the nude for artists if you approach it with a clean mind', she maintained.

In her case the law agreed with her and she escaped a criminal charge. Harold Spry, the fun parlour manager whose mind was perhaps judged less clean, was awarded a small fine for displaying objectionable material, although it was revealed soon after that nude peep show films were also being shown in two fun parlours in the city. Chief Secretary Baddeley, Police Commissioner Mackay and Lord Mayor Bartley said they had no power to stop these films unless it could be established that they were obscene. According to the law, this would involve someone entering the arcade, spending a penny or two, then claiming in court that they have been deeply shocked by what they had voluntarily paid to see.

COURTESY OF MOIRA CLAUX

Moira Claux in flight.

In later life Moira Claux became an accomplished dancer in the expressionist style, at one stage studying under the formidable Madame Bodenweiser of Kings Cross. She toured South Africa and India with the Bodenweiser ballet company. Taller and more muscular than the ballerina stereotype, she preferred to dance barefoot. Some of her favourite dances were based on the movements of Sudanese warriors. She even performed, barefoot but fully-clothed, in the premiere of John Antill's ballet *Corroboree* in 1954. In the audience were Queen Elizabeth II and the Duke of Edinburgh, on their first Australian tour. In less than seven years, Moira had worked her way up from the dark corner of a Manly fun parlour to performing before the Queen.

Throughout this period she continued to model, notably for photographers Max Dupain and Laurence Le Guay, and to challenge existing moral standards in other ways. In 1951 she announced her intention to appear as Lady Godiva in a parade through the streets of Dubbo (a nice idea even if this never eventuated).

She married twice and brought up four children. When I first met Moira Claux in a Maroubra café she was a charming, 70-year-old grandmother. She still displayed the powerful presence that clearly emerges in stories about her as a brash 16-year-old. Her brief appearance as the star of a banned peep show film was now a faded memory, largely overshadowed by her later appearance in one of Max Dupain's most beautiful portraits, *Moira*. She still works occasionally as an artist's model to pay the bills.

Her strongest impression of the period is that she, and the other group of bohemians who gathered in Kings Cross in the early 1950s, lived in an island environment. The world they built was so remote from the norm that they could have been living in another country, or so it seemed. They even created their own moral stan-

An innocent Shirley Beiger. The moral message was clear.

dards. She, for example, thought nothing of going to parties and dancing naked in the middle of the room, or of taking the late night tram to Redleaf Pool on a hot night and skinny-dipping with a group of friends. Often as not, a charismatic young radio actor named Peter Finch would be among the group of actors, artists, dancers and models living a life that might seem risqué even today.

Casual sex and group sex took place, although Moira says she preferred to fall in love with a man before going to bed with him. This was despite having more sexual opportunity than most teenage girls. Her liberal parents had given her permission to bring lovers home for the night.

This previously undiscovered world came prominently into public view with the sensational murder trial of Shirley Beiger in 1954. At the time, Shirley, a stunning blonde model and former Miss Australia contestant, had been sharing a poky flat in Kellett Street, Kings Cross, with her boyfriend Arthur Griffith, a bookie's clerk. On the evening of 9 August, she waited out the front of the Chequers nightclub in the city and shot him in the head. At the trial she claimed that she'd been driven to the point of desperation by her boyfriend's series of relationships with other women. He was 'a player', perhaps the first time this expression had entered the public domain. And she maintained that Arthur Griffith had expected her to accept his right to play around, as he appeared to be doing with a showgirl on the night he died.

When the jury was asked to accept that she had only wanted to warn him, not shoot him, they did. Shirley Beiger walked free and the moral message was clear. What girl wouldn't threaten to shoot a mongrel who demanded the right to have sex with other women? But throughout the trial Shirley Beiger's morality, as much as her intent to murder, was questioned. Her lawyers made much of the fact that, while she occasionally modelled swimsuits and lingerie, she was a very decent girl who wouldn't pose in anything less. Fortunately for her, the prosecution were unable to find photos that indicated otherwise.

This underworld was also exposed during the political scandal involving Russian consular official and spy Vladimir Petrov. Throughout the involved process that resulted in Petrov and his wife seeking political asylum in Australia in 1954, it was revealed that the mysterious Dr Michael Bialoguski, a Sydney medico and occasional member of the Sydney Symphony Orchestra, had groomed Petrov for defection by introducing him to the manifold pleasures to be found in Kings Cross. Visits to nightclubs and private parties were frequent.

In *The Petrov Story*, a book Dr Bialoguski wrote after the Royal Commission into the affair, he tells of one such encounter at the Potts Point flat of Alan Clarke, a dentist with diverse political affiliations. Despite being married, Clarke always referred to his circle of women friends as 'my harem' and when Bialoguski and Petrov said they would love to meet them, he surprised them by agreeing to this request. A harem night party was arranged in which everyone should come dressed according to the theme. Bialoguski paid a visit to the J. C. Williamson theatrical hire department.

> 'I am dark, wear a beard, and with a fez could pass as an Egyptian in the eyes of the uninformed', relates Bialoguski. 'Petrov, with the fez on his head, needed no further embellishment; he looked every inch the Eastern potentate, Egyptian or Turkish.'

Also playing the part were Alan Clarke, his obviously open-minded wife Joan, and three attractive young women introduced to guests as Marie, Mary and Joan. Dressed for the occasion, they performed their roles as harem girls with apparent enthusiasm, even fulfilling the fantasies of Petrov, a man generally regarded as socially obnoxious.

> 'He pinched one young woman here, another there, but all in a place which I'm sure made sitting for all a painful process for days to come.'

It has been reported elsewhere that during further research into the state of Western decadence, Petrov made frequent visits to

Kings Cross brothels. Once seduced by the bright lights, Petrov found he couldn't return to the monochrome world of Soviet communism. His defection was inevitable and he signed the official papers, appropriately enough, in a flat ASIO owned in the Cahors apartment block in the heart of Kings Cross, just across the road from where the El Alamein fountain now stands.

Another 1954 scandal confirmed that Australian society was perhaps not as comfy and conservative as it might have appeared from the outside. Leonard Lawson was a successful Sydney artist famous for drawing *The Lone Avenger* and *Hooded Raider* comic strips. He also took photographs for a few of the girlie magazines and in this capacity was able to act out his private fetishes for bondage and pornography. After hiring five young models from an agency he drove them to a remote stretch of bush near Terrey Hills in Sydney's north. Here he produced a sawn-off shotgun, tied the girls to trees, forced them to undress and raped two, including a 15-year-old. He assaulted the other three before, curiously, releasing them and calmly driving them back to the city in his Volkswagen. He submitted passively when arrested.

At his trial Lawson attempted to prove that the girls were willing participants, suggesting that they had led him on by openly discussing their own sex lives. Photos of the girls in cheesecake poses were produced to suggest that their morals were already loose. It was a cowardly defence and the jury didn't believe Lawson. The artist was given the death sentence, later commuted to 14 years in prison. Almost as shocking as Lawson's actions, at least according to some newspaper reports, was the evidence that there were young women in Australia, some under the age of consent, who were happily posing for the kind of semi-naked photos produced in court.

Kings Cross in the early 1950s was such a small world that it seems possible that the paths of the many diverse characters mentioned above must have crossed at some time. Dr Bialoguski played violin with the Sydney Symphony Orchestra under the leadership of Eugene Goossens. There was a rumour, never proved, that Goossens was somehow involved with the Petrov affair. It seems inevitable that at some stage Petrov visited one of the European cafés where Moira Claux performed her wild tribal dances. Did the sadistic Leonard Lawson ever visit masochist Roie Norton (the witch of Kings Cross)? It's tempting to see all these personalities intertwined in the manner of a television soap opera even if, in reality, they probably never met. 'No, I never met Shirley Beiger', said Moira Claux, 50 years after the event. 'Who was she?'

Evidence of immorality? One of the cheesecake photos produced at the trial of Lennie Lawson.

# chapter **ten**

# Battle of the bikinis

**F**rench engineer Louis Reard is credited with inventing the bikini in 1945, something he achieved, according to legend, by tying together four handkerchiefs at his kitchen table. Once sewn together the two pieces were small enough to fit into a matchbox, and this was the packaging gimmick used in Reard's Paris boutique. He also claimed that a true bikini should be able to be threaded through a wedding ring.

His choice of the name 'bikini' was topical. According to most reports, the name was inspired by the atom bomb testing at the Bikini Atoll in the Pacific. Another Frenchman, the Cannes-based couturier Jacques Heim, should also be given a share of the credit. At around the same time he created a swimsuit called the Atome which he promoted as 'the world's smallest bathing suit', at one stage hiring a plane to write this slogan in the sky. Reard retaliated by hiring another plane which wrote, 'Bikini … smaller than the smallest bathing suit'.

The first photo of a bikini (sometimes referred to as the French swimsuit or French costume) being worn was taken on the banks of the Seine in June 1945. It would be considered daring even today. The brave model was Micheline Bernardino, a dancer from the Casino de Paris, chosen because she was used to wearing even less on stage.

The first recorded sighting of the French swimsuit in Australia was barely four months later in George Street, Sydney. Here, on 11 October 1945, a *Daily Telegraph* newspaper photographer snapped 22-year-old Tivoli showgirl and model Patricia Niland wearing a costume on loan from the Mark Foys department store. She was helping to promote the Black and White Artists and Models Revel at the Roosevelt Cabaret that weekend.

The impact was immediate, according to the next day's newspaper.

'Tram-drivers stamped on their bells, motorists blew horns, and men whistled', claimed the report. 'A man fell out of a tram trying to get a better look.' There was a mixture of shock and disbelief from the crowd.

Pat Niland would later claim that her coat had accidentally slipped off as she crossed the road. More likely, this was a carefully staged publicity stunt, as was her next, even more sensational appearance in what would soon be known as the bikini. This happened two weeks later in the unlikely location of the old Sydney Sports Ground where Lionel van Praag, the 1936 World Speedway Champion, was promoting motor-cycle racing around the oval.

On the afternoon of 27 October, Pat Niland made her second public appearance in another bikini, this one a pink number with blue flowers.

It's 1945 and Patricia Niland models the daring French bikini at the Sydney Sports Ground. She was charged by police.

She posed for the cameras on a speedway motorcycle and did a speedy parade lap on the back of a midget racing car. Hers was a comparatively modest version of the outfit Michelene had worn in Paris, yet Miss Niland was charged on the spot with offensive behaviour by Sergeant Albert Caldwell, who was among the 8000

spectators at the speedway. He claimed that several in the crowd had objected to the swimsuit, yet was later unable to produce one name. Van Praag was also charged with having aided and abetted the offence.

There's a strange case of synchronicity at work here. Pat Niland was the sister of novelist D'arcy Niland who was married to the aforementioned Ruth Park. It is generally believed that Park's novel *The Harp in the South*, which generated such controversy a year after this incident, was based largely on the Niland family home in Tudor Street, Surry Hills.

A sensational court case took place at the Central Summons Court in late November in which the defence counsel, Mr Mulray, seemed determined to ridicule the arresting officer, at one stage holding up a replica of the offending costume in front of his own expansive frame and asking if Sergeant Caldwell still considered it offensive.

The bikini produced in court was described by the *Truth* newspaper as 'two flimsy pieces of material, scarcely a yard in all, when correctly adjusted became known as a French bathing suit, and when worn, cover only those portions of the female form which modesty, or the law, forbids exhibiting to the public gaze'.

In fact, it was the legality of the swimsuit that was on trial here. Mr Oram SM pointed out that there was no suggestion that Miss Niland had made any action or gesture that was offensive, so the case depended entirely on whether the wearing of the costume itself could be considered offensive. He quoted the *Oxford Dictionary*'s definition of offensive behaviour as 'conduct which gave offence or was likely to give offence', elaborating that such conduct might be 'displeasing, annoying or insulting … a breach of law, of duty, of propriety, or of etiquette'.

Patricia Niland walks into court, carrying the offending bikini in a small parcel. Exhibit A, your honour.

It was a very broad legal minefield that Patricia Niland had stepped into. Mulray pointed out early on that the overall outlook on such matters was rapidly changing and, to prove his theory, produced a costume commonly worn on stage by showgirls. A bizarre comparison took place in which the offending swimsuit was shown to have a greater expanse of covering material. Yet showgirl costumes were not considered offensive. No argument from Oram on that point.

'I quite agree with that and it seems to me that one has now to judge the matter according to the manner of living, the ideas of society and the general conditions prevailing.' The judge acknowledged that attenuated costumes were now being worn on beaches but such costumes might still be considered offensive if worn elsewhere, providing his own dramatic example of this. 'No one will deny that if a woman in a bathing suit of any description went into a church it might be considered offensive', he said. A speedway race meeting must have been considered closer to a church than a beach because, after due consideration, Niland and van Praag were each found guilty and fined 10 shillings with 8 shillings costs.

The incident proved to be a personal disaster for Pat Niland who obviously found the verdict unfair. Interviewed after her conviction she said she couldn't understand why, if it was offensive for her to appear at the sports ground in this swimsuit, it was not also considered offensive for models to appear in similar costumes at a Government-sponsored war loan rally in Martin Place. This rally, in which she had not appeared, had taken place without any criticism from the public.

After the trial Niland was given the nickname 'Eve in Eden'—a tag that made it increasingly difficult for her to find serious modelling work. She worked as a magician's assistant and was asked mainly to model lingerie, if not less. Throughout her life she blamed the bikini scandal for ruining her career.

Today, her eldest daughter, Barbara, still finds it hard to believe that her late mother had done such a thing.

'That's not the woman who was my mother', she says. Once married, Patricia Niland was so strict that she stopped her three daughters from wearing bikinis, even in the 1960s when these were considered normal beach wear.

Those first public displays of the bikini set the pattern for the next few decades. This scandal, rather than stopping sales of the product, encouraged women to buy. A Mark Foys' representative said later that summer, 'we've sold hundreds, and we're still selling'. They were selling even if these swimsuits couldn't be worn in public, well not by women.

In 1946 Bob Dyer, the portly host of the popular 'Can You Take It?' radio show, wore one on Bondi Beach as part of a promotional stunt, along with contestant Jack Rosen who won 25 pounds for taking up the dare. A reported 100 000 people were at the beach to see Dyer and Rosen parading on the sand in French swimsuits. This was seen as harmless fun yet at the same time women wearing bikinis were ordered off the beach at Dee Why, Clovelly and Coogee.

The unknown girl who had tried to wear 'an abbreviated French swimsuit' at Bondi Beach was mobbed by hundreds of beachgoers before she could even reach the sand. Shortly after this incident, another bikini wearer, 17-year-old Pat Riley, was escorted from the sands by Waverley Council beach inspector Aub Laidlaw, the first of his many personal evictions. After changing, Miss Riley threw the offending costume to the crowd who tore it to pieces. Others, including visiting Hollywood star Jean Parker in 1951, were also turned away. Most of these early attempts were publicity stunts, with photographers and newsreel cameramen ready and waiting.

These first appearances set the tone for a series of bikini battles that lasted for several decades and culminated in the late 1970s when women demanded the right to sunbathe topless on beaches.

This process was fought all the way by council-appointed beach inspectors, acting as self-appointed moral guardians and social commentators.

'Despite the trend overseas I don't think the bikini will ever be allowed at Bondi', predicted Laidlaw in 1953, who would become famous as Bondi's bikini *bête noir*, staging a personal battle against the increasingly smaller designs.

The bikini had also taken off in Surfers Paradise, which would soon become its spiritual home.

Paula Stafford began making swimming costumes in a former kiosk on Southport Beach. She is usually regarded as Australia's first local designer of bikinis. Her gimmick was to make them reversible, so the wearer had two swimsuits in one. Some of her first designs were made from shower curtain material. Helene Walder, a former cabaret singer, was another pioneering Gold Coast beachwear designer.

In 1952 Ann Ferguson, a model, was wearing a Paula Stafford creation on Main Beach when inspector Johnny Moffatt supposedly ordered her to cover up. When Stafford heard about the incident she sensed a golden opportunity.

'So I made five more bikinis the following day and five other girls wore them on the beach. I invited the authorities along—including the mayor who approved the costumes (though he later had trouble with his wife over the matter, I believe) and the chief of police who gave his OK. From then on anything brief could be worn.'

A re-enactment of this incident was recorded by Cinesound newsreel cameras and shown around Australia under the title, 'Beach Inspector's Battle of Bikinis'. Thanks to the controversy, Stafford's one-woman business grew until she moved into a factory employing over 50 workers. Her annual fashion parades in Sydney were a highlight of the social calendar. In 1955, Averil Roberts, aged 18, won the Miss Bikini contest at the Sydney Trocadero nightclub. She was wearing a Paula Stafford bikini and won a seven-day holiday to Surfers Paradise.

The bikini quickly became a symbol of sin, even attracting criticism from the pulpit. Father Shannon of St Vincent's Church in Surfers said, 'the bikini type of costume often worn here lowers the dignity of Catholic womanhood'.

By this stage the fame, or notoriety, of the Surfers bikini had spread around Australia. There were those who came to Surfers just to be able to wear a bikini that would have been banned anywhere else.

'It is a common sight to see parties of girls from Brisbane arrive on the Gold Coast by car—dressed as they left home in "approved" ordinary swimsuits to reveal brief bikinis underneath,' writes John Valder and Fred Lang in *The Gold Coast Book*. 'All of this seems to prove that whatever the wowsers say, it is girls who insist on stripping off to the bare minimum when they can do it without a beach inspector ordering them off the beach.'

Bikinis were also ordered off Manly beach, although less often than at Bondi. In 1954 a blonde sunbather, 'widely known at Manly because of her beautiful figure' was asked to leave by beach inspector Dick Battingham, who said later that hers 'was the briefest costume I've ever seen'. She left without argument.

The initial beach bans were depicted in the press as light-hearted fun, although it soon became obvious that a kind of moral battle had begun between women wanting to show as much skin as possible and conservative male officials who wanted to stop them. This resulted in countless examples of double standards. One of the most significant is mentioned in Damian Johnstone's biography of Johnny O'Keefe. In 1955 the man they called 'The Wild One' was encouraging his then girlfriend Marianne Renate (they later married) to pursue a career as a model. But when he saw photos of her in a bikini, he abused the photographer and demanded that these shots never appear in print.

'He said the photographs were too provocative and he wasn't going to have his girlfriend appear like that in a magazine for other men to drool over', Marianne recalled.

Coincidentally it was JOK's father, Ray O'Keefe, who was Mayor of Waverley during the period when bikinis were being most vigorously banned from Bondi Beach. He was a strong supporter of Aub

*Get off the beach! You're obscene. (1961)*

FIRST APPEARED IN THE BULLETIN, 14 OCTOBER, 1961. REPRODUCED BY COURTESY OF ACP SYNDICATION.

Laidlaw's campaign, based on his interpretation of Waverley Council's Ordinance 52 (Costume)—a law first passed in 1935.

Section (b) stated that: 'in any case where an inspector is of the opinion that any person's bathing costume is indecent or inadequate, or that the material thereof is too thin, or is not in a proper state of repair, or is for any reason unsuitable, he may direct such person to resume at once his ordinary dress.' The wording gave the inspector almost total discretion over what people wore on the beach. If he considered any costume unsuitable (or made of material that was too thin), he could order them off the beach. If they refused, under section (c) the inadequately dressed culprit could 'with any necessary force, be removed to the dressing enclosure or shed by the inspector'. The definition of 'necessary force' would be subject to debate in the summer of 1961.

The battles of the bikini took place on the beaches but also in the tabloids and on the newsreels. No summer was complete without at least one skirmish, more than likely a set-up on a slow news day.

Although Laidlaw took his job as moral enforcer seriously, he was also happy to ham it up for the cameras. In one Cinesound news-reel, events from Australia's first beach inspectors' dinner are shown. Seventy beach inspectors attended the function which included a parade of the new season's beach fashions for women. The swimsuits shown were all modest one-piece numbers, until ... 'Uh, oh, there's something happening here—and you're right, it's a bikini, the inspector's nightmare'.

Aub Laidlaw, moral guardian of Bondi Beach.

As the other 69 inspectors twirl invisible moustaches in silent movie expressions of lust, Aub Laidlaw, dressed in the comic opera uniform of his profession—panama hat, blue singlet, Persil white walk shorts and bare feet—springs onto the stage and grabs the miscreant.

On another occasion he interrupted a television interview with a bikini babe, grabbing the microphone and telling the viewers what he thought of her costume before ordering her off in the direction of the dressing sheds. Laidlaw was blessed with a sense of melodrama.

Part of the problem was the sleazy image that the bikini had unwittingly earned for itself. Featured predominantly on the covers of racy magazines and cheap novels, the bikini became a symbol of loose morals and a source of bad jokes: 'Tell me, is that girl wearing a black bathing suit or is that a bruise on her hip?'

One magazine, *Australasian Post*, became synonymous with the bikini, first featuring one on the cover in 1949 and continuing this theme for nearly 40 years. The magazine folded shortly after it changed its image. This publication, along with rivals like *Pix* and, briefly, the much more raunchy *AM*, were closely associated with barbershops. In the 1950s no salon was complete without a stack of *Post* or *Pix* for the exclusively male clientele to flick through while waiting for the regulation short back and sides.

Not all councils were anti-bikini. As early as 1955, the Manly Chamber of Commerce began to actively support the rights of women to wear two-piece costumes. At that stage an archaic local law dictated that swimming costumes must cover the front of the body from the armpits to at least three inches below the top of the legs. This meant that virtually everyone on Manly beach was technically in breach of the regulations, including the beach inspectors.

The Chamber of Commerce suggested that the best way to change the law would be to set up a test case using a volunteer wearing a typical bikini. She would be removed from the beach and prosecuted. Mr Peachey, president of the chamber, said his intention was to bring Manly in line with current dress standards in England and the Continent.

'We are not seeking sensational publicity or siding with indecency', he said, 'but we feel indecency, like beauty, is largely in the eye of the beholder, and that we should not have to dictate what the public shall wear or not wear for the sake of a few prurient minds'. Mr Peachey raised the point that it was a Manly identity, William Gocher, who had first challenged the law forbidding public bathing in daylight in 1902.

In response, Manly Council formally agreed to allow bikinis in 1955. It was a smart move that helped make theirs the most popular beach in Sydney.

Bondi was not so tolerant and by 1961 the joke had worn thin. Women now wanted to determine for themselves how brief their bikinis should be. Tensions arose when 75 girls were removed from Bondi Beach in one weekend alone, including a dancer, Joan Barry, who decided to take the matter to court after failing to supply her name and address to Aub Laidlaw. She alleged that Laidlaw had 'manhandled' her, using more force than necessary.

Previous bikini incidents may have been portrayed as

Yep, looks like three inches on the hip. Even old Aub would have approved of this bikini.

harmless fun but this case was taken very seriously with Mayor O'Keefe offering legal assistance to his frontline officer. This was more than a moral issue, this was a challenge to council authority.

In court, Detective Sergeant Baret described the offending bikini as being at least five inches below the navel and only three-quarters of an inch deep at the sides. This was a massive two and a quarter inches less than the three inches that Laidlaw had decided was the legal limit. Joan Barry was fined a minimal amount for calling the Beach Inspector 'a fool' but, more importantly, the Judge also fined Laidlaw for exceeding the limits of his powers. This landmark case inspired amendments to many Local Government Acts and from now on bikinis were officially tolerated in most areas of Australia.

During this period of debate, some women still supported the conservative side. June Dally-Watkins, Sydney's high priestess of deportment, drew up her own code, declaring that bikini bottoms should have at least five inches of material at the sides and descend no lower than an inch below the navel. The cups of the bra should be separated by material no less than two inches deep. Even Patricia Niland's 1945 bikini had measured less than this.

The artist Thea Proctor also disapproved, saying she objected to the bikini on both moral and aesthetic grounds. 'It cuts the figure in three and accentuates what it is meant to hide', she said. 'It is ugly and suggestive.' Even Annette Kellerman, the woman considered a pioneer of permissiveness after being arrested in 1907, was critical. She said in 1961 that bikinis gave her 'the shivers' and that she wanted to hang her head in shame when she saw some of the more extreme styles being worn.

Not everyone agreed with these public figures. In the correspondence files at Waverley Council is a handwritten letter from J. Goodman of Parkville, Melbourne, who supports the bikini on religious grounds.

'The Bible states that in the beginning God created the heavens and the earth', he, or she, writes. 'No government or council or individual or group of individuals has any right whatsoever to say what any person shall or shall not wear on or off any beach. If a person chooses to wear a bikini swimming costume that is their choice and no one has the right to interfere. There is not any such thing as an indecent costume. The Apostle Peter said, "Don't be meddlers" which is what those who object to bikinis are.'

While Mayor O'Keefe's replies to most letters are included in the files, this one remains unanswered.

Even after the Joan Barry incident there were still occasional reports of women being ordered out of beachfront cafes or banned from beer gardens. Five Sydney dancers, booked to appear at a Brisbane hotel, were evicted from the hotel's pool because of the brevity of their bikinis. One of the dancers, Myra Marsh, claimed that the same costumes had been worn on Sydney beaches without problems.

On the Australian bikini brevity scale, Surfers was at the top, Sydney came a close second and Brisbane was way down the list, somewhere near puritanical Melbourne where, in 1963, a girl photographed in a bikini on Brighton Beach was suspended from her school.

One of the more bizarre hits of that period was 'Music to Watch Girls By', a cheesy novelty song with vocals by Andy Williams. It celebrated the phenomenon of 'bird watching', as perving was euphemistically referred to in those hazy pre-feminist days. Perving was also the subject of several articles in pseudo-sophisticated magazines. In the December 1963 edition of *Man* magazine reporter Michael South penned a story entitled 'Beauty in the Bay', subtitled 'a symposium conceived for the noble art of bird watching'.

The Bay was Sydney's exclusive Double Bay region.

'It is the spot', notes South, 'where most of Sydney's dancers, theatrical artists, models, actresses, writers, TV personalities, beatniks, unmarried executives, playboys and the smarter office girls tend to congregate.'

And if you can believe Michael South, most of these human categories, including the beatniks, congregate in bikinis 'at the slightest indication of warmth in the air'. According to the photos illustrating his article, bikinis far briefer than the ones that had been evicted from Bondi Beach were now being worn without fuss in Double Bay. South observed the following in The Strip, the main shopping area.

'A particularly attractive dancer of the higher echelon wears a pair of hipsters and a bra-top with the closeness of a second skin. A model saunters by with hip-hugging shorts and a blouse with ignored buttons. An actress who is going for a swim, anyway, decides to do her shopping in the appropriate bikini.'

This was the strange irony of the Bondi Beach bans.

While beach inspectors were furiously ordering girls off the beach, girls wearing far less were strolling unconcerned through the shops of Double Bay where, according to the law, they could only be challenged if a member of the public reported them to the police. Waverley Council's regulations clearly stated that their inspectors only had jurisdiction over swimwear worn on the beach. Which meant that Laidlaw couldn't stop a girl, even a naked one, if she was 50 metres away along Campbell Parade.

Inspector Aub Laidlaw remains a mysterious figure in this period. Usually cast as the villain (he was once described as the 'tyrant of the tides'), he nevertheless received thousands of letters of support when he was asked to retire after 33 years patrolling his beloved Bondi Beach. It was estimated that he had personally made 6000 surf rescues in that period and was justifiably awarded a British Empire Medal for community services. Yet it was his vendetta against the bikini for which he remains chiefly remembered, at least by the hundreds of girls he evicted from the sand, sometimes using a little more force than necessary.

In 1975 he was interviewed and appeared to have mellowed.

'I was just doing my job', he said. 'In those days a certain degree of decency was called for. I used to insist on the bottom part being three inches wide but a G-string would do today.'

Girls going out to swim
Once dressed like Mother Hubbard;
Now they've got a different whim —
They dress more like her cupboard.

Aged 62 and still a regular swimmer, he was happy to be photographed with two local beach beauties, Julie Ismay and Kerry O'Brien, both wearing bikinis about half the size of the ones he was banning a decade or so ago. He thought these ones looked fine and even admitted admiring the topless sunbathers who were just starting to appear on the secluded parts of Bondi and Tamarama.

While they lasted, the bikini bans helped make Bondi Beach world famous. A trip to Sydney without visiting Bondi became unthinkable, although some commentators found the well-publicised display of flesh anti-climactic.

'There is an extraordinary difference, for instance, between the atmosphere of a beach at Sydney and a beach in Italy or the south of France' suggests John Douglas Pringle in his 1958 book *Australian Accent*.

This was the supposed difference: 'In Australia there is no eroticism: the handsome, sun-burnt girls play vigorously in the surf or lie on the sand and watch the young men riding the great Pacific waves in to the beach.'

We should take Pringle's erotic evaluations with a grain of salt, or sand. He was a dour Scot who came to Australia to be the editor of the *Sydney Morning Herald*. Among the glowing back cover blurbs from fellow newspapermen, my secondhand copy bears the scribbled comment 'Pommy Bullshit'.

Pringle does quote another opinion, that of English playwright Ben Travers, who had also made the pilgrimage to Bondi. Travers remarked on 'the magnificently proportioned young males with bronzed torsos, escorting an equal number of young females, who revealed, so far as the regulations allowed, that their forms were as attractive as their faces.'

Travers was happy to admit that he found Bondi sexually stimulating.

After being told by his Australian host that 'they only come here for hygiene and relaxation, there isn't a man or a girl on this beach with a thought of sex in their head', Travers replies: 'You can't say that now, I'm here for one.'

On the sands of Bondi, there seemed to be a competition among women to see who could get away with wearing the least amount each year, with Aub Laidlaw and his pals acting as impromptu adjudicators.

It's an interesting thought. Without the prowling presence of Laidlaw would women have been as committed to wearing less and less each year? Today censorship advocates are more subtle in their approach, well aware that the more tightly something is regulated, the more people will want to do it.

# chapter **eleven**

# Freak show

Throughout the 1950s strip shows, as we know them today, were not allowed in most Australian cities. One of the first legal displays of naked female flesh was the 1952 tour of the celebrated Folies Bergère troupe from Paris. Some performers appeared nude above the waist, but the rule was that they had to appear as motionless 'living statues'. Such scenes, usually referred to as tableaux, were always dimly lit. The local Tivoli Theatre circuit usually featured living statues in their variety shows and some female performers specialised in this technique, being able to control their breathing for minutes at a time. These performers were highly-prized as life models and Norman Lindsay, for one, was a regular hirer of Tivoli girls at his Bridge Street studio.

As revealed in *Madness After Midnight,* Jack Glicco's book on the London nightclub scene, there were also showgirls who were available—usually for large sums of money—to perform naked at private parties. There is anecdotal evidence that this service was also available in Australia, although stripping in a nightclub or any other public place was a crime normally rewarded with a prison sentence, as Kings Cross identity Luba Shishova found out in 1957.

A reporter had once tagged her 'The Olga from the Volga' because of her love of foul language and her constant threats to remove her clothing if she wasn't given money. It was a novel form of blackmail that usually worked.

During one typically tempestuous weekend, which began promisingly enough with her getting married sometime on the Saturday, Luba performed two impromptu strips after proprietors refused to hand over money. One was on the footpath in front of the Moka coffee lounge, the other outside the popular Hasty Tasty restaurant. A detective reported that Miss Shishova (or Mrs Wiley as she claimed she was legally called at the time) danced for the patrons at the Moka with her skirt pulled high above the waist. It was noted that she was not wearing underwear.

Her repeat perform-ance at the Hasty Tasty at noon on Sunday was observed by a passing reporter for the *Truth* newspaper.

Stage nudity was permissible, but only if the performers pretended to be statues.

'Luba started blistering the paint-work with her language, and then, standing athwart the main entrance, she repeated her strip tease as at the Moka—same words, same music.'

These acts of indecent exposure were part of a raft of other minor offences she committed over the weekend, which included the throwing of two large pot plants at a man, smashing leadlight windows, stealing a phone receiver from a private hotel and, as always, using offensive language.

Newspapers gleefully reported that Luba turned up drunk at Central Court, legs unshaven, smoking and wearing a skimpy polka dot bikini-style ensemble. She explained that this was what she was wearing when she was arrested so this was what she would wear in court. She received a nine-month sentence from Mr Bott SM. It's not clear what percentage of that sentence was inspired by her illegal strips.

For those not living in Kings Cross during the Luba Shishova period, it was most likely for a young Australian male to see his first actual naked woman, or the illusion of one, down in sideshow alley. This subsection of the entertainment industry appeared to have a moral code of its own. A performance that might have been banned in a city nightclub was somehow tolerated in a tent in Rockhampton or Kalgoorlie. In 1957 writer Eric Sapengro travelled with a typical sideshow community through Queensland and was especially taken with the performance of Paula Perry, a veteran showie who did a fan dance.

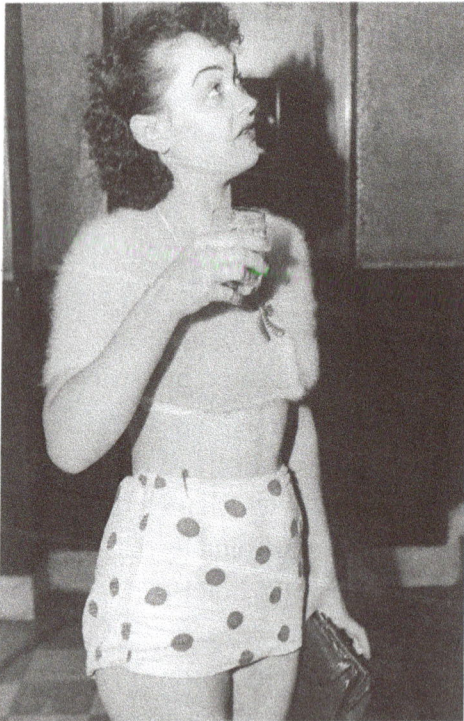

The Olga from the Volga, Luba Shishova, in her court costume.

'Paula struts on stage to a gay accompaniment, peels off her gloves, blouse and tight skirt, then finishes her strip-tease behind a screen so transparent it leaves nothing to the imagination. As the music changes to a dreamy tempo, she reaches overhead to a pair of white ostrich fans hanging on the wall and whirls out from behind the screen into a skilful fan dance. Paula's is one tent show that has every house packed out', adds Sapengro whose report appeared in the 17 April issue of *People* magazine.

He noted that several attempts had been made to ban Paula's performance, but each time Agricultural Society investigating committees ruled that the dance was 'artistic and in no way objectionable for public display'. They might not have been so lenient if the same performance was taking place in their town hall.

Another variation on this theme was the bubble bath act in which the performer danced, stripped, then took a bubble bath, sometimes asking a member of the audience to come up and scrub her back. There was one notable attempt to have this show banned at the 1956 Melbourne Show but, after due consideration, authorities declared it neither 'crude nor vulgar'.

During this period performers like Valescar the Ice Girl, The Girl in the Goldfish Bowl, Electros the Glamorous High-Frequency Girl of 100 000 Volts and The Eastern Snake Girl drew large crowds largely because they performed in various stages of undress. Bernice Koppel, born in Scotland, was the Eastern Snake Girl who 'danced in a bikini with a cobra in each hand and a python around her neck, playing with death and with men's emotions' according to the press of the day. As mentioned in Richard Broome's and Alick Jackomos's 1998 book *Sideshow Alley*, her act was seen as both exotic and, for the time, perverse.

'The spectacle of an attractive girl dancing with, to most people, repulsive reptiles is something men find hard to resist', they

Sideshow alley strip-tease.

A shower on stage was a new spin on the old bubble bath act.

suggest. Bernice reported that some men would stay for hours, paying four shillings a session over and over.

'It's good for business, of course, but a girl feels a bit uncomfortable when a man stands in the tent, hour after hour, just staring at her', she said. Electros had a similar effect. During her performance she shot out sparks from her body and was able to light a globe held between her lips or power a neon tube. Valescar the Ice Girl would simply be observed squeezed into a small compartment constructed from blocks of ice, her bikini the only protection against hypothermia.

These and other sideshow attractions depended largely on the rare opportunity for men to have a perve. Perhaps there was more to it than that. This was the only legal way for many men, and perhaps some women, to experience what we now describe as the sexual underworld, one that can now be openly seen on daytime television courtesy of Jerry Springer and Co. What was on show back then was real or imagined sexual kinks.

For example, the spectacle of a semi-naked tattooed woman sitting on a chair was enough to guarantee a steady stream of open-mouthed punters. Miss Cindy Ray was perhaps the best known of the tattooed ladies to tour the sideshow circuit, billed as Miss 3D, Miss Technicolour or, 'the lady who put the "oo" in tattoo'.

Her act consisted of allowing the public to come inside the tent and inspect her body which was completely illustrated from shoulders to toes. She wore a bikini but some demanded to see more, offering her handfuls of cash to see the tattoos that were hidden. She always refused.

She said that being on show was an unnerving experience, mainly because to most she was seen as a freak, if not a sexual deviant. At the Adelaide Show in 1963 a man appeared in the tent with a magnifying glass, convinced that she was a phony. Another man tried to scrub off the ink with soap and water. When she retired from sideshow alley in 1964 she wrote a book, *The Story of a Tattooed Girl*, in which she exposed the secret sub-culture of tattooed women and their male admirers. She also set up a mail order business selling a Miss Cindy Ray newsletter and individual colour photos of herself and other illustrated women in daring, for the time, poses.

Descriptions of these poses appeared in her newsletter:

ABOVE: 'The spectacle of an attractive girl dancing with...repulsive reptiles is something men find hard to resist.'

BELOW: There was also a niche market for tattooed women; Miss Cindy Ray strikes a pose.

'Me taken amidst an arrangement of pink tulle. Head and shoulder shot. Chest, shoulders and arm tattooing showing'. She adds a personal comment: 'Too candid for my liking. Otherwise I suppose it looks like me.' She also sold photos of models displaying the then little-known fashion for pierced noses. 'A very pretty girl poses in a head and shoulder picture wearing a silvery white wig hat and a small gold ring in the left side of her nose.'

Another Melbourne tattoo artist, Dan Robinson, estimated that by the mid-1960s he had performed about 25 nose piercings at his Williamstown studio. He had also begun to pierce men's ears.

Cindy Ray's newsletter reveals glimpses of the small but significant cult for tattooing and piercing that existed in Australia in the 1960s.

'Another Melbourne lass called Eve Lane had both sides of her nose pierced as well as her ears—she once had waist length brown hair which has recently been cut off. She is a very pretty girl within herself and attracts a lot of attention. Eve is an extremist with a growing taste to be really "way out" in make-up and jewellery. Recently I saw her wearing penciled eyebrows, blue eye shadow and blue lipstick, with her brown hair bleached white and tinted blue'.

Stevie Dane was another Melbourne woman who had her chest decorated with entwined roses, leaves and swallows and had both sides of her nose pierced.

'Apparently she does a little part-time modeling', writes Cindy Ray. 'Her waist length silver white hair makes her look picturesque.'

This was still a very private passion. In 1966, when *Australasian Post* did a feature story on the tattoo cult, every model except Cindy Ray appeared with their faces blanked out. She said that even she was uncomfortable about showing her tattoos in public.

OPPOSITE: Near nudity was acceptable when performed tastefully on stage.

When she went out in daylight she had to fully cover her arms and legs to stop people pointing and staring and, as often happened, people asking her what sex she was. She could only go swimming after dark.

The sideshow circuit was perhaps the only niche in society where such extremes of behaviour were tolerated. This also applied to the showies' personal lives. During Eric Sapengro's visit he witnessed the engagement of Merv Sheridan, aged 36, to another member of the troupe, 67-year-old Ma Henson. They later married with the blessing of the sideshow fraternity.

In the mid 1950s acts featuring deformities of birth were still part of Sideshow Alley, but were already on the verge of extinction. The most famous of these were Dave Meekin's celebrated pygmy displays. 'Strange and fascinating little people imported from Darkest Africa … see these exponents of poison arrows and deadly blowguns from jungle and desert … here are little men and women that never grow up …'

The pygmies were more likely to be African-Americans afflicted with dwarfism, who would sometimes agree to file their teeth to complete the illusion of savageness. Ubangi was the best known of Meekin's so-called pygmies. When in Sydney she stayed at the Hampton Court Hotel in Kings Cross and enjoyed a day's shopping in the city.

Also on show in Australia in this period were Tam Tam the Leopard Man; Anna John Budd, a half-man, half-woman; Jo Jo the Dog Faced Boy; and The Quarter Boy, a young man from America whose body stopped at the waist. According to Eric Sapengro's story, The Quarter Boy was the last of the real physical deformity acts to be allowed into Australia.

It's uncertain whether such acts were banned by official pressure or by a diminishing lack of interest from customers, but this positive act of censorship took place without any reported public protest.

# chapter **twelve**

# **Moral devastation**

Throughout the twentieth century, a variety of popular enter-
tainments were blamed for corrupting the morals of the young
and vulnerable. In the Second World War period, moving pictures
were the most quoted source of decay, even ones that had already
been filtered through the intense war-time censorship net.

'There is no doubt that this is an intensely sex-conscious age,
and it is unfortunate that sex-consciousness is so often stimulated',
writes Sydney University lecturer Zoe Benjamin in her 1944
booklet, *You and Your Children*.

'Children are permitted to go to any film on Saturday after-
noons, for example, the parents taking no care to find out if the
film is suitable. It may be a thoroughly good film for an adult,
but most undesirable for children. Week after week the young-
sters go to pictures of sophisticated adult life, the plots centre
around sex relationships; in many they see sex appeal
exploited; they witness all kinds of episodes (harmless enough
for adults) which emphasise sex; they see prolonged embraces,
with the result that their sex-consciousness is being played
upon week after week, month after month, from the time they
are small children; and at puberty they begin to make a definite
physical response which they do not understand, but which is
predisposing them towards early sex indulgence.'

The films she is talking about here would have included *Gone
With the Wind*, famed for its prolonged embrace.

Comic books were also considered a threat.

Peter Coleman, in *Obscenity, Blasphemy, Sedition*, records that by 1934 around 100 000 American 'pulp' magazines —'so called because if they were not dumped somewhere they would be returned to the paper mills for pulping'—were being exported to New South Wales each month.

'This poison must be kept out of Australia', editorialised the *Sydney Sun*.

This 'poison' included dime-store novels, *True Confessions* magazine and even the best-known syndicated comic strips. The ethnic diversity to be found in strips like 'Mandrake', 'The Phantom' and 'Tarzan' was singled out for attack in a pamphlet published by the Sydney Cultural Defence Committee, an offshoot of the Fellowship of Australian Writers with what appears to be a racist agenda.

OPPOSITE AND ABOVE: Moral dilemmas were portrayed in the pages of cheap romance novels. The wowsers disapproved.

'The Negro and his African jungle form no part of our national heritage and consciousness, and we will not have him here, neither in person nor by proxy through the permeation of his culture', threatened the anonymous author.

'Evil trash' and 'magazine offal' were other published descriptions of pulp fiction at the time. Special attention was paid to the true confessions-style of magazine as these were predominantly read by sensitive teenage girls. A list of story titles was released to warn parents, including: 'My Strange Honeymoon Experiences', 'Has Every Girl a Price?' and 'When I Went to his Room'.

An extract from *Love and Romance* was released … 'She turned her head suddenly and glued her lips to mine. It was a blinding nerve-wracking kiss.'

In 1938 a number of the pulps were banned by Customs. Reverend Brandt, a former Moderator of the New South Wales Presbyterian Assembly, was ecstatic at the decision, suggesting that the 'filthy and immoral American magazines' be burnt in a bonfire in the middle of Sydney's Martin Place.

The campaign continued after the war when a new breed of Australian-produced comics and magazines came under scrutiny. Typical of the genre was *Thrilling Detective* magazine, published in 1953 by Action Comics of Bond Street, Sydney. The stories were imported (or possibly stolen) from America, then repackaged with a spicy Australian-designed cover. These magazines featured a lethal cocktail of sex, death and even drugs. Stories in Issue One of *Thrilling Detective* included 'Stripped for Action', with references to 'reefer' cigarettes, and 'Heroin for a Heroine'.

By the mid 1950s Horwitz Inc., the leading publisher of Australian pulp, set up its own code of ethics to appease the likes of the Catholic Youth Organisation, which was blaming comics and crime fiction for causing an epidemic of 'moral devastation'.

Horwitz's grandly titled Associated General Publications Code of Ethics excluded any content which: '(a) glorifies or condones repre-

Pulp fiction of the 50s was seen as the root of all evil. Drug use and casual sex were common themes.

hensible acts or characters; (b) is offensively 'sexy'; (c) features illustrations which are offensively gruesome or 'sexy'; (d) distorts facts or is in any way misleading'.

Further stipulations were that all law-enforcement officers featured in their publications—'from park rangers to Police Commissioners'—should be portrayed as highly respected citizens and, 'at no time should a hero break any law e.g. when crooks are escaping from the scene of a crime, the hero must not jump into an unoccupied car which does not belong to him and give chase ...'

Furthermore: 'Any evidence of sadism or freakish moral tendency must be ruthlessly eliminated (e.g. whipping, torture, drug injection or any use of hypodermic or other medical instru-

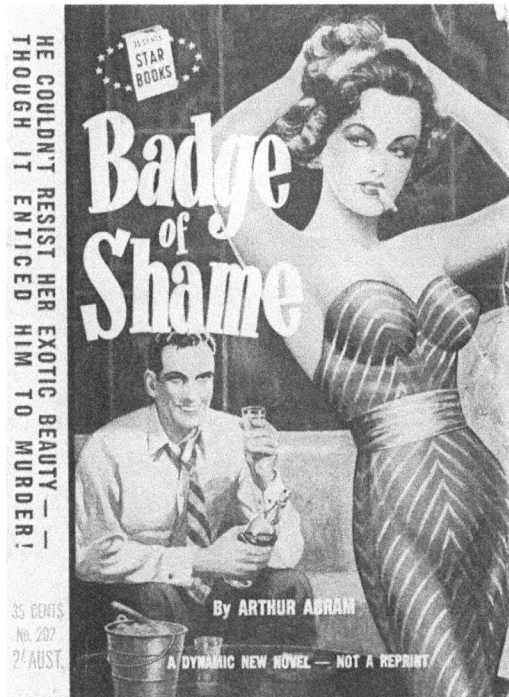

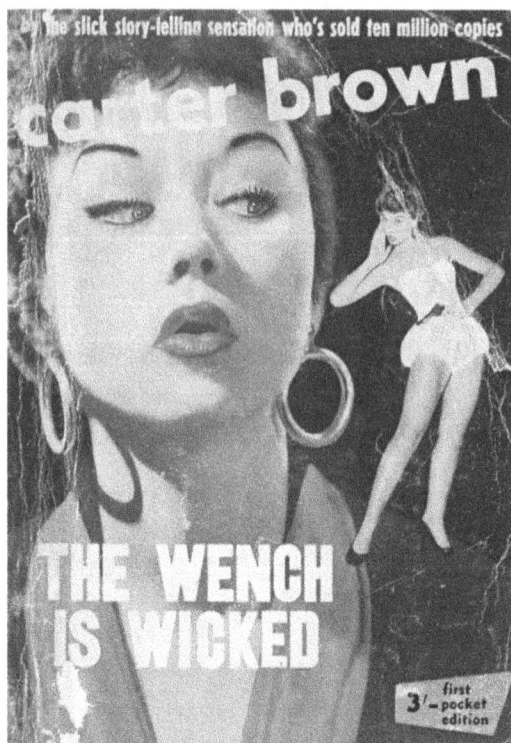

Australia's Carter Brown (Alan Yates) was our own king of crime fiction.

ment).' Profanity and 'double entendres' were also taboo.

Publications aimed at teenagers were even further restricted.

'There should be no reference to sex whatsoever in juvenile publications', warned the code. 'Where any female appears she must be properly and decently clothed. Divorce should be avoided as "unsettling to the teenage mind".'

This set of rules appears to have been studiously ignored by Horwitz's best-known author Alan Yates. By 1960 he had sold a claimed total of 25 million copies of his *Carter Brown* crime novel series. Writing from his home in the conservative Sydney suburb of St Ives, typical titles included *The Wench is Wicked, The Lady is Transparent, The Bump and Grind Murders, Nymph to the Slaughter* and *Nude—With a View*. All had sexy covers—but inoffensively so.

Here's a Carter Brown style sample from *Hot Seat for a Honey*, published in 1956:

> 'The door opened and a girl stood there. Black tight curls over her head and black eyes. A scarlet mouth slashed across her face. A black shirt so tight that the nipples made the apex of the triangular design. Black pedal-pushers, skin tight to mid-calf. Scarlet slippers with cream tassels. I blinked slowly. "A man!" she giggled.'

It comes as no surprise to learn that at least six Carter Brown titles were banned in Queensland, whose independent Literature Board of Review also prohibited a smorgasbord of Australian comics, plus lukewarm glamour magazines like *Gals And Gags* and racy tabloid publications like *Crowd* and *Weekend.*

One issue of *Weekend*, published in Sydney, was banned because it featured a photo of Hollywood actress Jayne Mansfield on the cover. The publishers wanted to know why and were told, in a Brisbane court, that it was her platinum blonde hair that was deemed offensive.

Mr Hart QC, the Queensland Review Board's counsel, attempted to explain.

'The build-up emerges with the other things and the dyeing of the hair. Some people with excellent morals dye their hair. However, it is a common thing among prostitutes to dye their hair.'

Apart from hair colour, behaviour was also under scrutiny. As early as 1949 there were indications that the current generation of children was acting differently to the pre-war generation. In *Watch Your Manners!*—a small booklet of social etiquette intended for Catholic youth—a variety of teenage temptations are discussed. Under the heading 'Modesty in Dress' comes a warning about the wearing of revealing clothes.

'Just as clean thoughts are more important than spotless clothes, so is modesty more important than style', writes the author Anne C. Tracey. 'A girl can't afford to wear daring dresses. Vulgarity in dress is as unattractive as vulgarity in speech. For a Catholic girl, it can be the occasion of scandal and sin.'

Other indicators of sin and scandal were as subtle as a seating position.

'If you wish to be a lady of manners, you will cross your legs below the knees, never above them'—and more—'a girl should never give the impression that she is on the warpath with vivid lipstick and fingernail polish'.

In conclusion the booklet warns of the dangers of what it labels 'teen-age rights' with specific mentions of such popular diversions as the jukebox.

The moral message is clearly stated by Anne Tracey.

Sleazy tabloids like *Weekend* were quickly banned, especially in Queensland.

'Court records are startling proof of these unfortunate boys and girls who seek thrill and excitement and eventually land in the clutches of the law. There is nothing in their heads and hearts and souls beyond what they put in their lives in childhood. Thoughtful boys and girls will do well to shun their company.'

Obviously not every teenager was thoughtful.

The golden era for 'boys and girls seeking thrill and excitement' in

Australia was the 1950s, or that's how it appears if you judge it by the volume of newspaper clippings. In the back rooms of most metropolitan newspaper libraries, where computer literate journalists dare not venture these days, chances are you'll find thick, dusty files labelled Juvenile Delinquency. Inside are fading reports of youth gone wrong, mainly in the late 1950s when there was a bodgie and widgie epidemic in most Australian cities. These teenagers—Australia's own version of England's Teddy Boys and America's Rockers—displayed a lack of moral standards that seems remarkable even by today's standards. Sin and scandal far exceeded Anne Tracey's 1949 warnings about vivid shades of lipstick.

Some examples.

June 1956: 'Adelaide detectives have been told [male] bodgies stripped and thrashed [female] widgies of their gangs for disobedience of gang rules.'

July 1956: 'One of the most shocking stories of bodgie depravity was told in Adelaide Juvenile Court this week by a 16-year-old girl. She said a gang of six young bodgies outraged her time and time again over a period of weeks, and used torture, terror and threats to make her submit.'

January 1958: 'A detective this week described a Newcastle sex orgy called "spinning the bottle" in which eight high school boys and girls, aged 13 and 14, had engaged.'

February 1959. 'A Sydney detective today told of a weird cult in which members were often scarred for life. During an orgy, he said, teenage girls were burned on the body with lighted cigarettes ...'

Exaggerated or not, such reports struck fear into the hearts of God-fearing citizens, to the point that Brisbane Police Commissioner Frank Bischof (the same moral enforcer who was also trying to stamp out pyjama parties in Surfers Paradise) set up a special anti-bodgie squad to control the hot spots in his domain. Special attention was paid to city milk bars where teenagers had taken to jiving on the footpath on hot summer nights. Bischof would have none of this and by 1960 when a world authority on delinquency, English clergyman Dr Maurice Barnett, visited Brisbane, he reported not one sign of misbehaviour in that city.

Perhaps he should have been looking in Parkes.

This country town 365 kilometres west of Sydney (best known these days for its telescopes and Elvis festival) was the unlikely location of one of the worst recorded examples of juvenile delinquency in Australia. Bad enough, or good enough, for Sydney tabloid newspapers to send out reporters by fast car to investigate in January 1960.

Exact details are sketchy but the tantalising phrase 'teenage sex nest' was used by *Daily Mirror* special reporter Gloria Newton. Two months previously, police had sprung 17 local teenagers who were taking part in a series of organised sex parties. Superintendent John Wright, the local cop

## "TORTURED" BY BODGIES

ADELAIDE, Thurs.—One of the most shocking stories of bodgie depravity and violence Australia has yet heard was told in Adelaide Juvenile Court this week by a 16-years-old girl.

### Young girl's grim story

The girl said a gang of six young bodgies outraged her time and time again over a period of weeks, and used torture, terror and threats to make her submit.

The almost hysterical girl, now pregnant, told the court the bodgies threatened to thrash her with a bicycle chain "spiked" with razor blades unless she "gave in."

They also tripped, kicked, knifed and robbed her, and had threatened to burn her with cigarettes if she talked to police about bodgie-widgie cult activities.

**"Not safe"**

The deeply-moved magistrate who heard her story said the girl would not be safe abroad until the gang was broken up.

Police said they believed the girl's story.

The girl had been charged before Magistrate Scales with being an uncontrollable child.

She was also charged with breach of a good behaviour bond granted her in the same court last year.

The girl, fair-haired and pretty, came from a good home, the court was told. Her parents, who were in court, wept as she told her story.

Mr. L. J. Colquhoun, of the Children's Welfare Department, said the girl's life had been made "an absolute horror."

A written statement allegedly made by the girl to policewomen C. Rudd, in which she explained how she came to break her bond, was tendered in court.

In it, she said that last February she began to go to the pictures by herself so as to keep away from boys.

One afternoon at the pictures she went out at interval to get a drink. She saw a group of boys whom she had previously seen around Adelaide, but whom she did not know well.

Two of them came over to her. One grabbed her arm and twisted it. Then another came up and told her to keep quiet, according to the statements.

She was pushed into a car in which there were six youths and, according to the statement: "Every time I asked where we were going I was told to shut up."

"They stopped down near Osborne, where there are no houses and told me to get out. They took off all my clothes and pushed me down on the ground."

**"Kicked"**

The girl said a boy who seemed to be the leader then demanded to know whether she would submit willingly, and when she said she would not, he kicked her in the stomach.

Others pulled out pocket knives, according to the statement, and flashed the blades.

The girl said she was then held down while the bodgies were intimate with her one by one.

"Then they flung the clothes at me and said, 'Put them on and shut up.'"

"On the way back in the car, the statement said, one of the youths said: "How's your little sister these days?'"

"They threatened that if I told anybody that they would get my little sister coming home from school.

"She is aged 10 years. I did not want her to get hurt, so I shut up about what had happened. I was terrified.

"Since this, about fortnightly, when I am walking along somewhere, these boys meet up with me, and take me somewhere.

"They have threatened me with bike chains with half razorblades between the links, and knives.

"They have burnt me with cigarette butts. They have slapped my face.

"I feel as if they are haunting me wherever I go," the girl's alleged statement said.

It continued: "They all wear black stovepipe trousers, black suede shoes, black-draped coats, pink shirts and black and pink ties.

"They all wear their hair long with side brows, and long in front.

"I have been so frightened that I have tried to kill myself.

"About three weeks ago, I took poison.

"I vomited quite a lot after taking it.

"Last Tuesday I tried to strangle myself with a sheet."

Det. Gollan, in charge of the drive against the bodgie-widgie cult in South Australia and Mr. Colquhoun said investigations were being made into the gang.

Mr. Scales, S.M., sent the girl to a reformatory, "for her own protection and safety," until she is 18.

Australia's bodgie gangs were portrayed as depraved sadists by the popular media.

Pray this isn't your daughter. Widgies, the female of the bodgie species, were usually depicted as morally slack she-devils. And they smoked in the street.

who had arrested several participants on various morals charges, described the phenomenon as the 'worse than animal-like activity of a certain group'. The activity was a series of gangbangs, to use more modern terminology, involving two girls and up to 15 boys. The girls, aged 14 and 17, were willing participants. The older girl was the chief organiser. The parties took place in the 14-year-old girl's home if her mother was away, or in parked cars if she wasn't.

Gloria Newton arrived in Parkes seeking graphic evidence of animal-like activity but was sadly disappointed upon arrival.

'Parkes is a quiet place at night', she wrote. 'Young people hurry to their destinations. But over the town hovers an air of waiting—of expectancy. The people are wondering if the uncovering of the teenage sex nest by the police has routed immorality among the youth of Parkes—or is it only the beginning?'

It was 8 p.m. She checked the main street but there was no sign of the Saints—the bodgie gang who had allegedly been responsible for turning Parkes into a suburb of Sodom and Gomorrah.

'The milk bars were deserted and no juke boxes blared into the hot stillness of the night', she noted. She was told that the juvenile problem began in the gardens surrounding the local swimming pool, but there were no parked cars there that night. Instead she went to the Town Hall where a council meeting had just finished.

The Mayor, Alderman Moon, was relaxing in his shirtsleeves over beer and sandwiches. He was not too happy to see Gloria Newton.

'No', he told her. 'We had nothing to say about the sex orgies tonight. There was a discussion about a gymnasium which we thought could help solve our delinquency problem. The sex orgy is a matter for the police. It is nothing to do with us.'

The mayor insisted that his was a good town and had been so for the last 35 years. Superintendent Wright, himself the father of a 17-year-old daughter, was a little more forthcoming.

'His face hardened as he described some details of the sex orgies', observed Gloria. One of those details was that the girls had carved their initials on their arms with razor blades.

'Their animal depravity sickened me', he said. 'The morals of a minority of teenagers in this town are rotten. Gradually the condition will spread unless the whole community takes a hand in cleaning up the mess.'

When questioned, the teenagers of Parkes said there was nothing to do in the town except go to the pictures two nights a week.

This incident also featured in a further story on teenage sexuality in *People* magazine in August 1960,

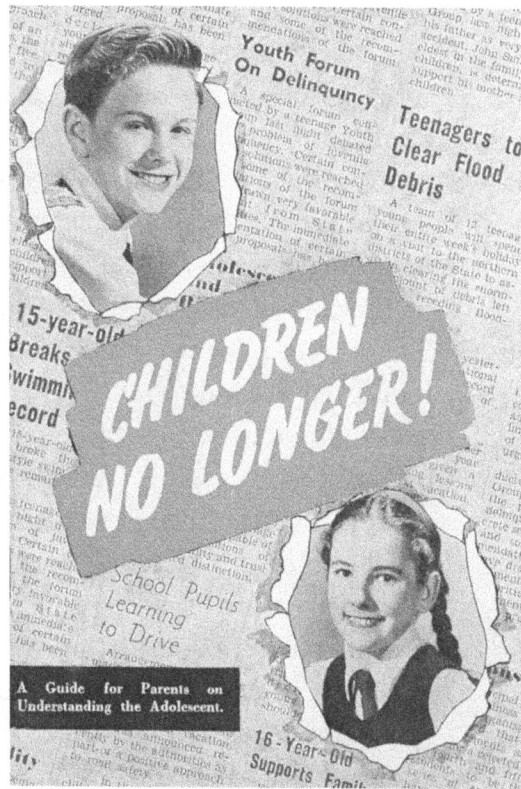

Responsible parents gave these booklets to their children upon puberty. The untamed kids of Parkes must have missed out on their copies.

along with another from a small, unnamed country town in Victoria. Here, at a school with only 18 pupils, the schoolmistress discovered that all but two of the children 'were not only indulging in sex exercises of one sort or another in the playground and on the way home from school but, were busy at sex play in the class room. After a lot of questions and a lot of vague answers she was able to fix the beginnings of this juvenile orgy on a girl of 12, obviously strongly sexed. She had seduced the boys and encouraged the girls.'

The only two pupils not taking part were aged six and seven.

Teenage, even pre-teenage sex, has probably taken place in

every generation but the most disturbing aspect of the bodgie and widgie approach, at least to moral guardians, was the age of the participants and the apparently organised nature of their sexual activities. It was noted that one of the regular members of the Parkes sex nest was a particularly advanced boy aged 12. He was the younger brother of the 14-year-old hostess.

There were also those S&M overtones. These were only ever hinted at in print but passing references to 'burning with cigarettes' and 'slashing with razors' were enough to get the message across to adults with fertile imaginations. This angle was highlighted in a 1959 report on activities in Parramatta in Sydney where 'scores of Sydney's dead-end girls are torturing themselves for the "honor" of belonging to self-mutilation cults.'

Police reported that the cult involved players pressing lighted matches and cigarettes to their skin. The first player to recoil from the pain was 'chicken'. Another fad down Parramatta way was the carving of boyfriends' initials on girls' bodies using knives, razor blades or ink-filled nibs. If none were available the phosphorous tip of a Redheads match, rubbed vigorously on the skin, would leave a semi-permanent marking.

'What to do about it all?' asked *People* magazine. One controversial suggestion was to not always treat the girls as innocent victims. Mr Justice Page of the Bendigo Supreme Court, asked to comment on the increasing incidence of carnal knowledge charges in his jurisdiction, said: 'A lot of the offences are due to the girls themselves. I am inclined to think we should be able to indict these girls as accessories, but the legislature in this State has not yet reached that state of enlightenment.'

It wasn't only bodgies and widgies who were participating in illicit sex practices at this time.

In March 1959, *People* magazine had reported that in Victoria alone police had seized more than 30 000 obscene pictures and transparencies, 'including a number taken by a Melbourne businessman that would have brought blushes to the cheek of a Port Said "filthy pictures" vendor'.

These photos were being sold to adults and schoolchildren. One set of five photos was reportedly doing a brisk trade among schoolboys, despite the stiff purchase price of 30 shillings. *People* magazine reporter Thomas Aubrey suggested that the main photographing and distribution centre appeared to be in Victoria where some of the models for the photos were 'practically household names', including entrants in beauty pageants.

Up to this point it had been assumed by authorities that most obscene photos were smuggled into Australia from the dirtier parts of Europe. Now it appeared that a thriving trade was based in marvellous Melbourne, and some of this local smut was obscene enough to be exported back to the sin capitals of the world, including Copenhagen and Amsterdam.

Discovery of the trade was made in 1958 when a Melbourne model, who willingly posed for artistic nude photos, was asked if she would like to pose for some shots 'with a man in a suggestive attitude' as *People* quaintly described it. She refused the offer and her boyfriend dobbed in the photographer to the police.

Two members of the Vice Squad got a search warrant and raided the photographer's studio. What they found there shocked even hard-boiled Melbourne coppers. Stacked in cardboard boxes were hundreds of photos of naked girls, some posing with naked men. Some of these girls were prominent local models identifiable through their more mundane work as department store mannequins. Instead of the drug-crazed widgies or toothless prostitutes that police might have expected, these were attractive girls from ordinary homes—some rather well-connected socially. The girl next door as someone surely put it.

The police officers also found a small book listing names and addresses of models, both male and female. The girls had been given a secret code number indicating how far each was willing to go.

This was just the tip of the immoral iceberg. Police soon discovered a surprisingly large network of studios churning out filth. One studio belonged to one of Australia's best-known portrait photographers. This sexual underworld shouldn't have come as a surprise to anyone who was a regular reader of respectable technical magazines like *Popular Photography*, where small ads down the back pages advertised slides and transparencies for sale. The code words were 'figure studies'.

In the August 1957 edition of *Popular Photography*, Squire Studios, based at a post office box in Crows Nest, Sydney, was inviting anyone interested to write for a free catalogue of their 'New, Exciting, Unique 35 mm. Natural Colour Transparencies'. It wouldn't have taken much effort by the Vice Squad to find out just how new and exciting these transparencies were.

NEW

EXCITING!

2 x 2 COLOUR SLIDES

Glamour · Pin-ups · Figure Studies
Also World Famous Paintings
reproduced in Kodachrome Colour

Write now for free and
post-free catalogue of these
Unique 35mm Natural
Colour Transparencies.

*SQUIRE STUDIOS*
BOX 32, P.O. CROWS NEST, N.S.W.

Nude (and possibly obscene) photos were not that hard to obtain.

A total of 23 models were eventually identified and questioned by the Vice Squad. Some said they had appeared voluntarily but, according to the prevailing moral guidelines, they were still regarded as innocent victims exploited by predatory males.

The proportion of girls who agreed to pose 'in a suggestive attitude' with a male or female partner was relatively small, but large enough to shock police. Some had taken the wise precaution of covering their faces, including the girl who featured along with a prominent Melbourne company director in photos described in court as 'the most shocking series of pictures ever to fall into the hands of the Australian police'.

The man, aged 30, had taken these pictures in a suburban bedroom using a camera with a remote control device which was clearly visible in some shots. He pleaded guilty to 23 charges relating to obscenity and was fined 520 pounds. According to the dirty picture code of ethics, he refused to name the masked girl involved in the most shocking photos but police easily identified another nine girls in his vast collection. One had been a finalist in a beauty pageant. Another had often featured on the cover of reputable magazines including knitting catalogues.

One of the more comical aspects of the case was the company director's penchant for taking photos of young women carrying toy pistols while wearing nothing but a large straw hat. A suitcase full of these and other props was produced in court.

In another in this series of court cases a photographer said he had met his model in the flat she shared with her mother. It was the mother who had encouraged her daughter to pose for the first rela-tively tame set of photographs. The man later persuaded the girl, according to the prosecution's version of events, 'to pose for a series of pictures in a descending order of decency'. At the bottom of this moral pile were photos of her with painted weals on her body, suggesting that she had just been beaten by a sadist. Others showed her posing with another young woman, each pretending to whip the other.

Although logic would suggest that the girl would have been at least a partially willing participant, the photographer was the only one charged. Police described him as depraved.

It was reported that police engaged in at least one sting opera-tion during this crack-down, persuading a prostitute who had been asked to pose to agree to the request. As photos were about to be taken the detectives burst in the studio door. Police stressed that while prostitutes were sometimes approached to appear as

Those forbidden wisps of pubic hair make this vintage nature study an obscene item according to pre-1969 standards.

models, the majority refused and were apparently eager to dob in photographers to the cops. According to their own moral code, they considered such individuals as perverts who deserved to be locked up.

As a result of the 1959 Vice Squad campaign, a total of 19 people appeared in Melbourne courts—businessmen, labourers, a truck driver and a tramways man, plus a showgirl. The role of this solitary female to be charged was not specified. All were convicted and one was sent to prison. A total of 1000 pounds in fines were issued. Towards the end of the sordid business, the chief of the Melbourne Vice Squad, Sergeant J. W. Dawes was convinced that his operation had barely touched the obscene picture trade in Australia.

'We are still just scratching the surface', he said.

These were true words. Just over a month later, in another Melbourne court, a magistrate asked for the lights to be turned down while 600 slides of naked Melbourne models were projected as evidence. The slide show took most of one day's sitting. Shortly after this case, another man was convicted of taking obscene photos of his wife and his ex-wife, separate and together. He declared in court that his wife wanted the photos for her own private collection. Despite the suggestion that many of the photos had been taken with the models' consent, the magistrate determined that this man 'was debauched, eager to debauch others, and willing to use people already debauched'. He was imprisoned for three months.

The prevailing mentality here was that obscenity was basically a male crime. Inspector Healey, officer-in-charge of the Vice Squad, explained his department's moral position for the benefit of *People* magazine readers.

'The men who make and traffic in the photographs seek new and more abominable perversions', he suggested. 'The girls who pose are led into immorality. They find it hard ever to truly respect themselves and their bodies again. Young people who see the photographs cannot help but be affected. Their minds are inflamed and unbalanced and their whole lives can be ruined.'

We'll have to take his word for it. Material deemed to be obscene and confiscated by the various Vice Squads around Australia is still kept safely under lock and key. Evaluation by the general public is forbidden nearly 50 years after the crimes were committed.

This includes the aforementioned 'most shocking series of photos ever to fall in the hands of Australian Police', as well as a series of indecent matchbox covers seized from a shop in Elizabeth Street in 1958. The proprietor, Lazar Kolt, admitted in Melbourne's City Court to having sold thousands of the enamelled covers before being stopped. Constable Murphy, who made the arrest, said that while he was speaking to Kolt in his shop two boys, both minors, came in and asked to buy some covers. Mr Daly SM examined 15 different covers, all featuring captioned illustrations produced in Sydney, before declaring that five of the drawings were obscene. Kolt was fined 21 pounds.

In this climate even saucy seaside postcards were under threat if a member of the public found offence.

But reading between the lines, there emerges a distinct impression that Melbourne *circa* 1960 was a much more vibrant city than is indicated by John Brack's celebrated painting, *Collins St., 5 p.m.* (1955), of its citizens grimly walking along the street. Melbourne was also the home for an Australian subdivision of bohemia, as wild in its own way as Kings Cross.

The male of the bohemian species was noted for his duffel coat, corduroy pants, suede shoes and general air of anarchy. He favoured hair longer than the norm, a sharp jazzer beard and possibly smoked a pipe. The female favoured either long straight hair or the gamin look made famous by the actress Jean Seberg. She wore voluminous jumpers, tight matador pants and chain-smoked Gauloises.

Among this group were the fabled beatniks, a cult briefly popularised by *Everybody's* magazine—'50,000 Australians who don't believe in anything' claimed their 1960 front cover. The core element were arty anarchists who were commonly thinking that there had to be more to life than 9 to 5 suburbia. Perhaps their most eloquent spokesperson was Barry Humphries, a disciple of Dada who created his alter ego Edna Everage in the late 1950s.

Melbourne bohemians frequented acrid coffee houses to listen to folk music and trad jazz or went to poky art cinemas to watch continental movies. They drove vintage cars, made sculpture from driftwood, drank Galliano and Turkish coffee. Included among this random assortment of ratbags and radicals were those who would later transform themselves into Liberal Party politicians like Athol Guy, or millionaire directors of advertising agencies like Phillip Adams.

It's easy to imagine that the models and photographers accused of peddling obscenity were also linked to this sub-culture, attracted by the sheer anti-Establishment wickedness of pornography. Or maybe they were just in it for the money, like Harry Hounslow of Adelaide.

Among occasional reports of the dirty picture trade in other states is one, dated 1956, of a 19-year-old 'shapely young blonde secretary (name suppressed)' who told Adelaide Police Court that she had placed an advertisement in a newspaper seeking part-time modelling work. Quick to respond was Hounslow, a 45-year-old salesman, who took her to a secluded spot in the scenic Adelaide Hills where he persuaded her to pose as nature intended.

'It came as a surprise to me when he asked me to take my clothes off in the scrub', she said, perhaps a little unconvincingly. 'He told me to put them on a rug which he had spread out. The photographs were taken against my will. He used a box camera.'

Hounslow must have had considerable powers of persuasion. He also talked her into taking a photo of him in the near nude, a snap which would later emerge as an interesting piece of evidence. In this case, the charge had less to do with the obscenity of the images than the photographer's subsequent attempt to extort money from her. When the poor girl phoned Hounslow a few days later she was told that the photographs had been shown to some men who worked with her father and 'they were very interested'. She protested and was told she could buy back the negatives for ten pounds.

Meanwhile, back in the sinful Sydney suburb of Parramatta, a 33-year-old labourer pleaded guilty to a charge of exhibiting an obscene publication. The publication was a series of pornographic photos which his 13-year-old daughter had removed from an unlocked drawer in his bedroom and taken to school to show the other girls in her class. The labourer said he had bought the photos from a man in the Woolpack Hotel. He was fined five pounds and the photos were confiscated.

# chapter **thirteen**

# Sex swaps

In November 1954, it was announced that Christine Jorgensen had signed with the Palladium Theatre circuit for a 16-day cabaret tour of Australia. This was shocking news at the time. Christine, born George Jorgensen in The Bronx and a former GI in the United States Army, had had the first recognised sex change operation in Copenhagen in December 1952.

When asked what she would be doing on stage during her proposed tour in December, promoter Harry Wren replied, 'Well, she's a terrific singer. She dances too and does a comical turn with the comedian Lee Whyler.' Wren described Jorgensen's singing style as somewhere between Marlene Dietrich and Greta Garbo.

Others saw it differently, suggesting that all she had to do was stand there while the audience, mostly 'more mature patrons' according to Amer-

Don't call me George. Miss Christine Jorgensen performs in 1954.

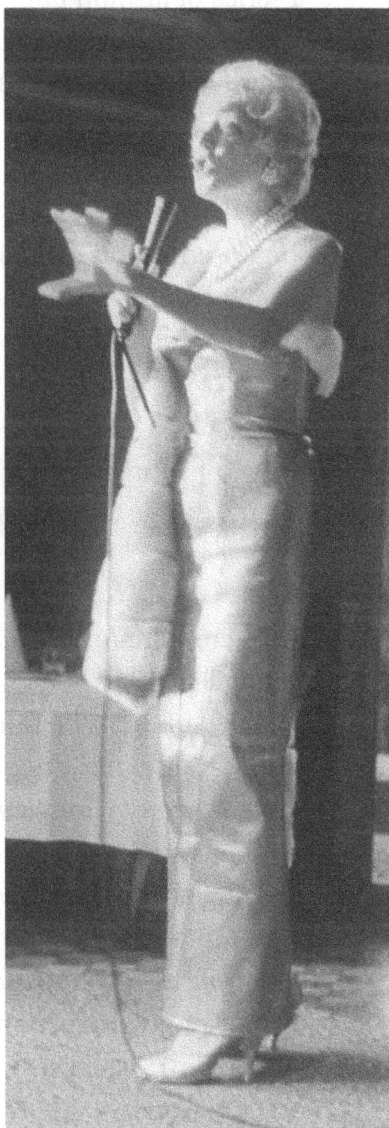

ican reports, sat and stared at her. Although she insisted her act was done in the best possible taste, the mere thought of a woman who used to be a man was obscene enough for several American cities, notably Boston, to ban her from appearing on their stages.

Sydney, too, seemed likely to follow that trend.

When it was announced that Jorgensen intended to headline a series of fashion parades (showing off her impressive collection of Paris gowns) June Dally-Watkins, the principal of Sydney's largest model agency, announced that none of her girls would be appearing.

'I'm sure the parents of my models would strongly object', she said in the *Daily Telegraph*. 'A fashion parade featuring Miss Jorgensen would reek of the sort of sensationalism that's popular in America but isn't suitable in Australia. For local girls to parade with him—I mean her—would lower our professional dignity.'

## Models boycott Christine's fashion shows (MAN-WOMAN IN SWIMSUITS)

There were more practical problems, as 19-year-old model Jan Mitchell pointed out.

'I'm certain I'd be terribly embarrassed and wouldn't be able to stop staring at her', she said, adding that 'if I did parade with her I'd want a separate dressing room'.

The issue was heated enough to inspire a public protest meeting in Sydney's Lower Town Hall, where church leaders and representatives of women's organisations and model agencies spoke out against the proposed tour. The protest was organised by Sydney radio producer Julien de Meyrick.

The *Sydney Morning Herald* also condemned the tour, but for other reasons.

'Must we have Miss Christine Jorgensen inflicted upon us?' an unidentified columnist asked. 'This person's sole claim to fame is that, formerly a U.S. soldier, her sex was changed a couple of years ago. An interesting medical phenomenon, no doubt. But who wants to gaze at her because of the physiological transformation that she underwent? To my mind, the public exploitation of such freakishness is degrading to show business.'

Their various concerns were resolved when Christine Jorgensen abruptly cancelled her tour, reportedly over the financial arrangements.

She did make it to Australia in July 1961, without any discernible protest, for a very well-paid four-week nightclub tour. Clutching the mandatory toy koala as she stepped off the plane at Mascot, she was described by one reporter as a 'tall, thin blonde wearing a form-fitting high neck frock, a three-quarter length mink coat and high heel shoes'. She was happy to admit that: 'without all the publicity I doubt if I would have decided on show business as a career'.

In 1961 it was still deemed illegal for a man to appear dressed as a

"What the —— —— are you staring at?"

Cross-dressing was common enough to be the subject of underground postcards, sold under the counter in pubs.

woman in a public place, and any transvestites found by the police were routinely beaten and locked up. This situation even applied after the launch of Sydney's famous Les Girls revue in 1963, where the drag queens had to change back into their male clothes after a show if they wanted to leave the premises.

There had been a small but established drag scene in Sydney dating back to the early 1940s, if not earlier. One of these war-period drag balls, the Gala Drag and Drain Party, is recreated in Jon Rose's obscure 1961 novel *At the Cross*. The ball was attended by eight Carmen Miranda impersonators, a Pola Negri, a Lana Turner, a Dame Nellie Melba and a woman dressed only in melted wax. The party was raided by gangs of police armed with truncheons. The book may be a work of fiction but I'm assured the details, including the police raid and the melted wax woman, are based on actual events.

Jorgensen managed to avoid the traditional NSW Police beating because she was legally a woman and had the passport to prove it. Still, it was mentioned that she avoided using public toilets while in Sydney, holding off until she could use one in her hotel or dressing room.

While men were not allowed to cross-dress in public, it was apparently fine for a woman to dress as a man. One of Sydney's best-loved entertainers of the pre- and post-war periods was jazz singer Nellie Small—a woman born in Australia of West Indian parents, who spent her entire adult life in male clothing. Brought up in Catholic orphanages, she was adopted by the Meggitt family in North Sydney. It was her adopted mother, Edith Meggitt, who first suggested she wear male clothing as a gimmick when she first appeared at a talent quest at the Gaiety Theatre in 1931. She won the quest and as she began to perform professionally at swank Sydney clubs like the New Cavalier and Romano's, a publicist recommended she wear male clothing all the time, something Nellie was more than happy to do.

Nellie Small lived openly as a man for most of her extraordinary life.

'The comfort of male dress appealed to her and for the past 25 years she has worn nothing else', reported *People* magazine in 1952. 'For street wear she has well-cut tweed and pinstripe suits; at home she wears slacks, shirts and men's comfortable cardigans or jackets. She wears a man's wristwatch. She has a weakness for gaudy ties and socks, which are chosen for her by Mrs Meggitt. Apart from her stage tophat, she wears no headgear.'

Nellie's choice of clothing caused only mild controversy, like the time she attended a race meeting while on tour in Auckland, wearing a man's suit with a lady's race ticket on her lapel. Her manager explained the situation and she was let in. In Sydney she had never had any trouble.

'But, although she has adopted a masculine air, along with male dress, it would be a superficial observer only who could mistake Nellie Small for a man', claimed *People* magazine. 'As she has grown older she has put on a little weight around the hips and there is something unmistakably feminine about her walk. Her voice, too, is not adult masculine. A listener, hearing her talk from another room, would probably guess that she was an Australian boy whose voice had not completely broken.'

Her hobbies were also masculine. She was a passionate punter and her idea of a good time out was to go to a friend's place for a beer and a game of poker. In another interview, after she had worn a dress on stage as a one-off joke, she responded to the suggestion that she might now wear them more often.

'Ah, don't be crazy pal. Wear frocks and give away all my privileges? I'd die if I couldn't go in the bar and have a few drinks with the boys occasionally.'

# chapter **fourteen**

# The knight and the witch

**S**ir Eugene Goossens' world crashed-landed at Mascot Airport on 9 March 1956, short-ly after stepping off the morning flight from London.

As the recently-knighted conductor of the Sydney Sym-phony Orchestra (SSO), he was accustomed to being waved through the baggage clearance room. On this occasion he was intercepted by Nat Craig, the Se-nior Customs Investigator, who asked Goossens to accompany him to the search room.

Here two detectives from the Vice Squad were waiting. They had received a tip-off that Goossens had been cruising the grubbier shops of Soho, buying up big on pornography.

After telling waiting reporters that he was feeling sick,

Anything to declare, Sir? Eugene Goossens shortly before his dramatic departure from the Sydney Symphony Orchestra.

Goossens was then escorted to another building where his luggage (one briefcase and six suitcases) was ready to be examined.

Inside were found 1166 photos, films, books, three rubber masks and, according to one version, his knighthood medallion.

*Eugene Goossens*

CONDUCTING THE

**SYDNEY SYMPHONY ORCHESTRA**

Goossens' impeccable social credentials only added to the scandal.

Eight hundred and thirty-seven of these photos would later be deemed to be obscene. Some of the photos were enclosed in sealed envelopes marked Brahms and Beethoven. The detectives then escorted Goossens to the Criminal Investigation Branch in the city. After another three hours he was finally allowed to leave.

When he arrived at the house he was renting in Burns Road, Wahroonga, the press were there waiting for him, as they would be for the next six weeks. Goossens' wife was overseas. After his daughter Sidonie came out to tell reporters that her father was confined to bed, they stayed on permanent guard duty outside the front gate, sleeping in their cars overnight. This was the biggest story in a decade.

On 12 March, Goossens formally announced his intention to resign from the SSO 'because of ill health'. A day later two customs officers arrived with a summons. Sir Eugene Goossens was to be charged under Section 233(1) (d) of the Customs Act 1910–1954, relating to the 'possession or importation of blasphemous, indecent or obscene works or articles'.

The maximum penalty was 100 pounds.

The case was adjourned to 21 March but on that day Goossens sent word that he was too ill to attend. He was found guilty in absentia and fined the maximum amount.

By now the scandal had taken on a life of its own.

The *Sunday Telegraph* reported that Goossens was implicated in 'black masses' and other forms of devil worship which they claimed had taken place in luxury homes in Sydney's North Shore and at a mansion near Katoomba. According to the newspapers, police were investigating these so-called satanic cults and more arrests of high-profile people, including some radio actors, would be made soon. They weren't.

Meanwhile Goossens remained a prisoner inside his luxury home. His employers, the Australian Broadcasting Commission (ABC), formally accepted his resignation on 11 April despite the personal endorsement of its chairman, Charles Moses (himself later to be knighted) who appeared as sole character witness at the court case.

One of very few others to publicly offer their support was Ron Smart, a trombone player with the SSO, who rode his bicycle all the way to Wahroonga to see his former conductor. Left in limbo, Sir Eugene Goossens finally did what he had no choice but to do. On 26 May, using the pseudonym E. Gray, he took a KLM flight to Europe, never to return to Australia. There were rumours that he had been given an ultimatum to go by the Cahill state government, with the proviso that if he ever returned he would face more serious charges.

There were also allegations of possible blackmail threats, hinted at by Goossens himself in a farewell message. Here he claimed, 'It is my misfortune that I allowed myself to be used to bring prohibited matter into this country as a result of persistent menaces, which I could not ignore without involving others.' He then thanked his friends for their understanding and confidence in him.

Jack Shand QC, hired by the ABC, had also referred to these threats at the court case in which he vainly tried to defend his absent client.

'One finds it almost impossible to reconcile the life of the defendant, which has been lived for a long time on a high aesthetic plane, with these very bad types of pornographic and salacious pictures which are exhibited in this case', he began. He then pointed out that the photos were great in number—'over 1,000'—and were in double envelopes and double sealed.

**NORTON**
"Not understood, not understood"

Rosaleen Norton was a veteran of the obscenity game, first charged in 1949.

This, Shand suggested, was an indication that the photos were not intended for his personal use. 'It will be revealed that these photographs were brought out as a result of threats, the nature of which will become apparent in later days—very soon I hope.' Goossens' solicitor, Mervyn Finlay, made a similar claim after Goossens' flight, hinting at an unnamed 'serious enemy' from overseas.

CIB chief, D. Calman, disputed all these allegations by saying that at no stage had Goossens mentioned blackmail threats to police.

But the above story is just one part of the scandal. If anything, a much more fascinating episode took place in a poky, foul-smelling flat in Brougham Street, Kings Cross. This was the so-called coven of the infamous Witch of Kings Cross, the artist Rosaleen Norton, herself a veteran of a series of obscenity charges.

As early as 1949 she had been charged under the Police Offences Act with having exhibited four obscene paintings at a Melbourne University exhibition. Charges were dropped after her lawyer argued that her drawings were mild compared with, for example, illustrations in *The History of Sexual Morals*, a book then freely available. 'We have to cater for people with normal reactions to sex', her lawyer argued. 'Not morons, the subnormal or neurotics.'

Nevertheless, Roie, as most called her, was considered abnormal enough at the time to be asked to undergo testing by a Melbourne University psychologist, L. J. Murphy. She happily agreed, sitting for a Rorschach-Behn test and a detailed session on the couch.

The results are included in Neville Drury's biography, *Pan's Daughter*.

'Roie had her first sex experience at the age of twelve. It had been "rather accidental", she told Murphy, "in that a boy of my own age suggested that we do it. I found it very painful and did not try it again …"'

Or, at least, not with him. Later in life she found she especially enjoyed the company of homosexuals, telling Murphy that 'those men are soft and rounded, and they let me do what I like with them—I enjoy most of all their hands softly running up and down my back—sometimes they use pencils and leaves'. She liked having sex with lesbians, although her main preference was for sado-masochism.

'She told Murphy she liked to be tied up and beaten, and to engage in sexual intercourse so powerfully that her partner would hurt her by forcing her back against the pole to which she was tied.'

With women, she took on the dominant role: 'kissing and being kissed, stroking and being stroked'. She confessed that she would like to have her own penis to have sexual penetration with a woman.

This must have been startling stuff for 1949, even to a trained psychologist. After due scientific analysis, Murphy concluded that his subject had both a superior intelligence and a tendency towards mental illness.

He wrote: 'there is a straining towards odd and original fantasies which is not completely realized: this suggests that the subject is really malingering in the direction of schizophrenia, that she is trying to be odd and peculiar, and to give way to unconscious fantasies'.

Her life seemed to follow this diagnosis.

Two drawings from her 1953 book, *The Art of Rosaleen Norton*— 'they wanted to bind it in batskin', claimed one newspaper breathlessly—were deemed 'obscene and an offence to chastity and decency' by a Sydney magistrate. One of those offensive paintings, entitled *Black Magic*, was found obscene for a second time when displayed in the Kashmir Coffee Shop in Kings Cross. This work, 'odd and peculiar' if you like, depicted a nude woman having sex with a black panther. The café proprietor David Goodman copped a five pound fine.

Perhaps only Dr Murphy would have not been surprised by Roie's next claim to fame.

Sometime in June 1955 some photos were taken of Roie and her then lover, the fragile poet Gavin Greenlees, indulging in what they called a Sex Magic ritual dedicated to the god Pan. The photos included one of what would later be described as an 'unnatural sex act' (anal sex in today's language).

The negatives were stolen from her flat by Francis Horner and Raymond Ager, two underworld characters who, unwisely in hindsight, offered them to a variety of Sydney newspapers for 200 pounds. The photos were obviously too hot to publish but the editor of the *Sun* smelt a big story and turned the two men over to the Vice Squad.

One of the officers to arrive and make the arrest was Detective Bert Trevenar who then decided to raid Norton's flat to arrest her and Greenlees on six charges, including ones of having assisted in making an obscene picture. According to one version of the story, while searching the flat, the officers found a bundle of letters tucked be-

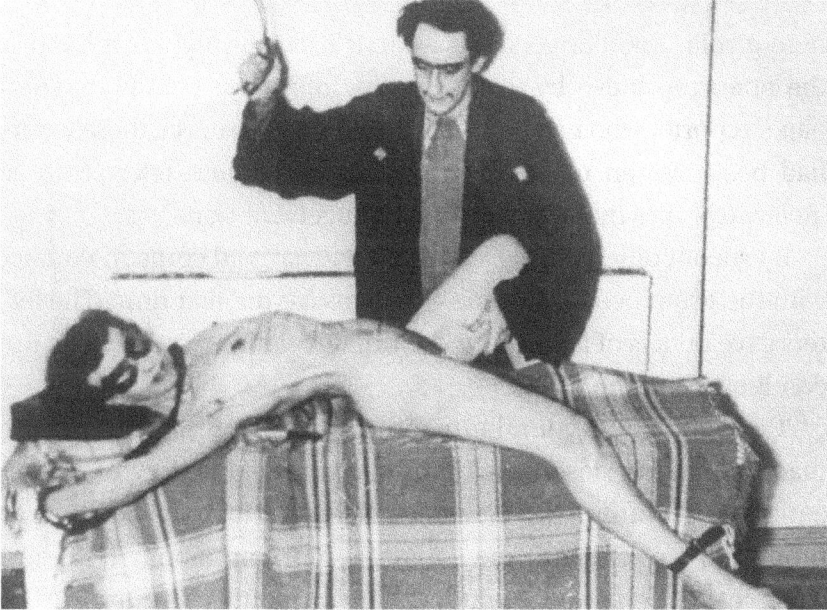

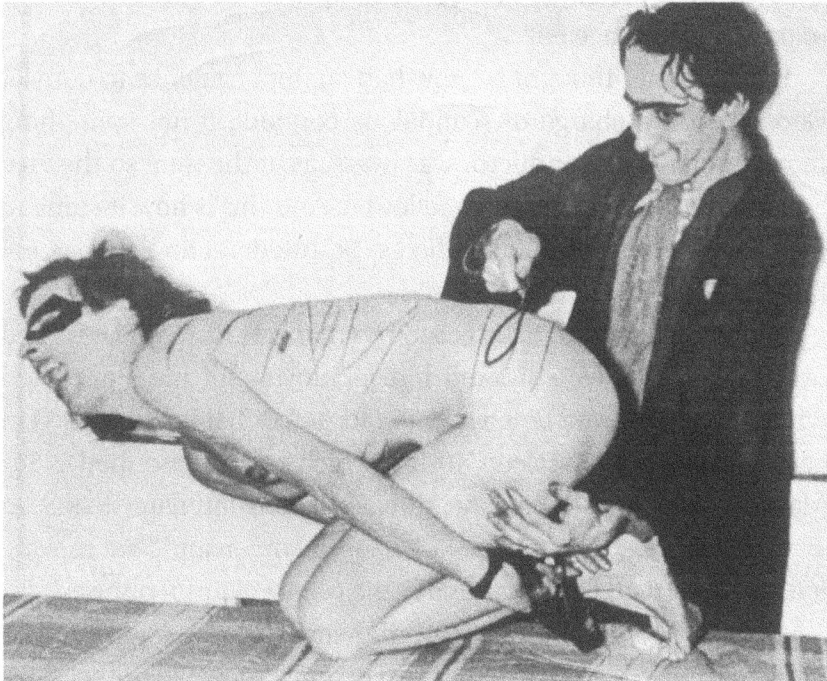

Sex magic or scandalous conduct? These photos of Norton and Greenlees were part of the proposed police case against Eugene Goossens.

hind a sofa. Another version says that Trevenar had been handed the letters previously by an anonymous informant, possibly a newspaper reporter who had himself stolen them. Whatever, these letters had been written to Rosaleen Norton, sometimes referred to as 'Roiewitch', by a man signing himself Eugene or Gene.

By sheer coincidence, Detective Trevenar had come in contact with the esteemed Sir Eugene Goossens for the first time. The letters gave details of an obviously intimate relationship between the conductor and the witch.

'Contemplating your hermaphroditic organs in the picture made me nearly desert my evening's work and fly to you by first aerial coven', ran one, typical of Goossens' literary style. 'But, as promised, you came to me early this morning (about 1.45) and when a sudden flapping window blind announced your arrival, I realized by a delicious orificial tingling that you were about to make your presence felt …'

Bert Trevenar thought he now had enough evidence to convict Goossens on a charge of scandalous conduct, if not something more serious. The conductor was overseas at the time so the Vice Squad arranged for him to be followed. And this is how it came to pass that a group of police officers, both federal and state, were there waiting for the plane to land.

After passing through the Customs grilling, Goossens was turned over to Trevenar who showed him photostats of the letters he'd written to his beloved Roiewitch. He admitted that he'd indulged in certain rituals with Rosaleen Norton, which he also described as Sex Magic. Under questioning he revealed some intimate details to Trevenar. 'I placed my tongue in her sexual organ and kept moving it until I stimulated her', was one of the more colourful phrases.

As well as what we now call oral sex, Goossens admitted to participating in some of the 'sex perversions' shown in the series of photos of Norton and Greenlees. The detective obviously thought he had just caught a very big fish but this scandal within a scandal was never proceeded with. Trevenar was told by the Commissioner of the Police that only the lesser Customs charge, relating to the importing of obscene photos into Australia, would be followed up. The decision to ignore the potentially more serious charge was supposedly made by the Attorney-General's Department.

In a 1999 story on the scandal published in *Good Weekend* magazine, Trevenar, then retired, said: 'A couple of people who were involved were pretty high up on the social [ladder] and the government of the day took notice of them. There's no doubt in my mind. That was the situation.'

As also revealed in that story, Trevenar kept copies of the police paperwork from that case in a cupboard in his home in the Sydney suburb of Ashfield. He also kept copies of the photos of Norton and Greenlees and of the letters sent to Norton by Goossens. It was obviously a case he could never forget and he remained angry that it was never fully resolved.

Some of those photos taken in Norton's flat might be considered hard-core, even by today's liberal standards. Others show an almost comic side, with Greenlees dressed in pantomime costume and fake moustache, and Roie, striped with fake blood, faking pain. Or is it pleasure?

You have to wonder. Are these worthy of the demise of a musical career? For your evaluation, two of the more subdued photos in the series are included in this book.

But what about the photos that caused Goossens his much more public disgrace? Filmmaker Geoff Burton interviewed Trevenar shortly before he died. The detective had only vague memories of the photos confiscated at the airport which were destroyed immediately after the court case (this was done according to protocol, although Goossens' daughter has suggested this as proof of a conspiracy).

Trevenar recalled lots of images of naked women being tied up, but one in particular caught his policeman's eye. It was a photo of a model wearing the top of a London policeman's uniform hopping astride a bicycle. It was obvious that she wasn't wearing underwear. What today might pass as a humorous postcard was then considered obscene.

Shortly after the Goossens scandal had dissipated, a strangely similar case involving Abraham Saffron was reported in the darker sections of Sydney newspapers.

In 1956 Saffron, then aged 36, was a well-known nightclub identity, known mainly as the proprietor of the racy Club Roosevelt. Although he liked to portray an image as a respectable Jewish family man, Saffron had an obvious flamboyant streak, exemplified by his fleet of large, black American cars bearing Australia's first personalised number plates. His own car, an imported black Pontiac, carried ABE 111. In one photo a group of bikini-clad showgirls are shown perched on the bonnet.

Family man perhaps, but there were persistent rumours about Abe, and veterans of the police beat were not surprised when, in October 1956, he was one of a group of men and women committed for trial on various charges of scandalous conduct. Saffron's brother Henry, a taxi driver, was also alleged with having 'openly outraged public decency by taking part in lewd, obscene, disgusting exhibitions'.

One of those exhibitions took place at a party in a house at Palm Beach on 24 June 1956, just a month after Goossens had been expelled. It was alleged that Abe Saffron, another man Hilton Kincaid, and an unnamed woman had engaged in scandalous conduct at the party. There was mention of the use of whips. Abe Saffron was also charged with committing an unnatural offence with a woman at Potts Point on 11 August. Saffron was further charged with being the occupier of premises at 44 Macleay Street, Elizabeth Bay, in which two obscene publications were found. A woman, described as a typist, was charged with having helped in the production of these publications.

The police prosecutor Mr R. Turner said that very grave matters were involved in the case and that evidence would show that Saffron was 'completely depraved and has no moral sense whatsoever'.

Here was a fascinating scenario in which it appeared that a small but organised group of men, ranging in occupation from tailor to labourer, liked to gather at a series of secret locations to watch 'lewd, obscene and disgusting exhibitions' take place between consenting adults. Photos were taken which were then published in book or magazine form. There was something of the billiards club about it all.

This had all the makings of a sensational series of courtroom dramas and the action began with the committal hearings at the Central Court of Petty Sessions in February 1957. A female witness fainted in the box as she gave evidence. She was part of a group of 11 men and two women—'one of them coloured' the *Sydney Morning Herald* felt obliged to report—facing a variety of scandalous conduct charges. Before collapsing, the witness told the court that she knew she was doing something wrong when she posed with another girl at Palm Beach. The next day another witness identified a woman in court as one of the two naked girls she allegedly saw Saffron hitting with a whip.

The gallery was packed and a large crowd of spectators gathered outside the courtroom. They were not to be disappointed. At the end of the day, one of the accused made a wild dash across George Street in an attempt to avoid photographers, knocking down an elderly man and narrowly being missed by a passing truck.

Abe Saffron's charges were listed for a separate October 1957 hearing. He was ordered to report weekly to police after the prosecution alleged that he had made arrangements to go overseas. This was strenuously denied by Saffron's solicitor who said that his client had arranged for his wife to take their son to Switzerland for schooling after the headmaster of his exclusive private school in Sydney had expelled the boy.

Another episode in this drama took place in November 1956 when a young woman was arrested on the streets of Brisbane. Described as a 17-year-old showgirl, she was charged in Brisbane Police Court with having assisted in the making of an obscene publication at the aforementioned Palm Beach party. She was remanded to appear in Sydney Children's Court on a morals charge.

But that was where the excitement ended. The Palm Beach case did not proceed when the prosecution was suddenly dropped. Saffron's unnatural offence charge was also dismissed and, after being convicted and fined a total of 20 pounds for being in possession of the two obscene publications, Saffron lodged a successful appeal based on an astute legal interpretation of the Obscene Publications Act, first drafted in 1885.

'The facts in this case are clear but the points of law are not so simple', said Judge Holden. 'The element of gain is essential for the success of such prosecution.'

No element of gain could be substantiated and the convictions and penalties were quashed. Saffron walked free.

# chapter **fifteen**

# **Pyjama parties**

In the late 1950s in Surfers Paradise, plumber-turned-property-developer Bernie Elsey made his name by staging a series of so-called pyjama parties at his Beachcomber Resort hotel in Cavill Avenue. The parties started in 1957 after Elsey saw a newspaper story which reported that Princess Margaret had attended a pyjama party in London. The parties began benignly enough until a woman wrote a letter of complaint to the Brisbane *Courier-Mail* and the parties instantly became front-page news. The usual angle was that these were pagan orgies thinly disguised by baby-doll nighties and shortie pyjamas. The revelries traditionally ended in the wee small hours with a conga line of men and women dancing through the streets in their nightwear, followed by a plunge into the hotel swimming pool.

Dirty dancing, 1960s' style. The pyjama party was seen as the depths of depravity by Queensland cops.

COURTESY OF ERN McQUILLAN

Such behaviour was wild enough to attract the attention of a section of Brisbane police, known popularly as the 'Flying Squad', who raced south in divvy vans for the thrill of arresting young women in wet nightwear.

While there was no law against people doing the conga in their pyjamas, the police managed to dredge up an old war-time restriction forbidding the drinking of alcohol in close proximity to a dance floor. But the real crime was obvious to Queensland Police Commissioner Frank Bischof, who described these pyjama parties as immoral. This was the same man who banned teenagers from dancing on footpaths in front of Brisbane milk bars.

The matter was raised in state parliament and even evangelist Dr Billy Graham, on his first national tour of Australia, was invited to preach against the dangers of pyjama parties.

If he hadn't known already, Bernie Elsey soon realised that scandal of any kind is the best publicity of all. He made sure that reporters and photographers were present when the police arrived and one almost suspects him of anonymously phoning the cops to complain. The Brisbane flying squad arrived with such regularity that any party that didn't end with a police raid was considered a disappointment.

The tone of newspaper reports of the period suggests that Surfers had now become Australia's regional office of Sodom and Gomorrah.

'Most of those at the party wore pyjamas, while some of the girls wore bikinis', observed a *Sydney Morning Herald* stringer, who reported to startled Sydney readers that many of the partygoers in pyjamas were underage (under 21 according to Queensland drinking laws) and that there was a lot of 'necking' going on. This was shocking stuff, ensuring that hordes of southerners were mentally booking into the Beachcomber for their next holiday.

Elsey made sure they would not be disappointed.

When guests arrived at the Beachcomber they would most likely be greeted by Bonnie Nelson, employed by Elsey as the manager, although her main function was as a kind of walking advertisement. Every day she took her two pet poodles for a walk while wearing high heels and a bikini so brief it would have been booted off the sands of Bondi. To complete the picture she and the dogs wore matching ribbons. To two generations of tourists, Bonnie Nelson was known as the Poodle Lady.

There were other reasons for Surfers becoming the sin capital of Australia. In the early 1960s, pharmacist Des McNamara erected an animated neon sign for Coppertone suntan lotion above his chemist shop.

Using the slogans, 'Tan, don't burn' and 'Don't be a paleface', the sign featured an illustration of a puppy dog grabbing the panties of a cute young girl. Up and down went the panties, exposing her untanned bottom. The girl depicted was three years old.

The veteran Gold Coast journalist Alex McRobbie says in his book, *The Real Surfers Paradise*, that the sign caused great controversy when first erected and some residents complained that it was indecent and should be removed. It was perhaps the first neon sign to be branded obscene.

'Interest in the sign was so intense' he recalls, 'that I was commissioned to take photos of it for newspapers and magazines around Australia which published them to reinforce the image of "sinful Surfers Paradise".'

Sin continued inside the chemist shop. In the days before The Pill, this shop was the main outlet for condoms in Surfers. It was open day and night and did a roaring trade in condoms during the holiday season.

Bernie Elsey, the man who gave Australia the pyjama party, has an even greater claim to fame. In 1965 he was fronting an independent group of Gold Coast retailers known as the Progress Association. His group was upset at council plans to introduce parking meters (gold ones) to the streets of Surfers, claiming that this would seriously affect retail trade. It was his brilliant idea to protest this move by sending out girls in Paula Stafford-designed golden bikinis to feed coins into meters that had expired.

152
banned

Far from being a council promotion, as people may suspect, the Gold Coast Meter Maids were an act of retail anarchy.

The pioneer Meter Maid who set out on 7 April 1965 was Annette Welch. It was no coincidence that she was a receptionist at one of the several Beachcomber motels that Elsey owned.

This bikini-clad protest resulted in the local council attempting to ban Meter Maids from the streets. A male parking inspector on a scooter followed Annette around on that first day in an attempt to scare her off. The council soon discovered that there was no law preventing someone from placing coins in parking meters; only from taking them out.

In fact Annette Welch decided not to continue after her first day on the job but a replacement was soon found and within a year there were at least two maids on permanent duty with a third touring interstate promoting Surfers as a golden retail opportunity.

With poetic irony, the golden bikini girls soon became the best-known symbol of Surfers Paradise despite the continuing efforts of various local authorities to kick them off the streets. Even Mayor Bruce Small, a man whose statue now stands in the heart of Surfers, was against the Meter Maids, partly because it wasn't his idea. He started his own rival group of promotional girls but these were soon ignored. The people, and the tourists, wanted the original golden girls.

There were also objections on legitimate moral grounds.

'The image depicts women as objects who are wanting sex', suggested Rosemary Kyburz, a Liberal member of Queensland Parliament. 'It downgrades every woman who lives on the Gold Coast and attracts the criminal and undesirable element in the area.'

She may have been right, but in the end it was modern traffic regulations, not censorship, that resulted in the demise of Meter Maids in their original format. In 1988 the last remaining Progress

OPPOSITE: Annette Welch was Australia's first Meter Maid, if only for one day.

has been raised in a perverse atmosphere where the word is considered ugly. But if it is a lewd, coarse sound, then I want to evoke it to do away with the banal and the dishonest.'

Having completed perhaps the first serious discussion of the word 'fuck' to appear in a mainstream Australian newspaper, it was reported that Lenny Bruce calmly ate a pear. He said that he had been charged for using the word once before in San Francisco, but was found not guilty.

After being banned by the management of Aaron's Exchange Hotel, the Australian Broadcasting Commission also banned him from appearing on the 'People' television program. Bruce was scheduled to appear in an interview lasting 24 minutes with host Bob Sanders. After this was cancelled, Sanders said he strongly objected to the board's decision, indicating that the comedian had agreed to pre-record the segment and have any obscene language deleted.

'I had hoped in this interview tonight to present to Sydney people the real Lenny Bruce—not the monster that they have been led to believe he is', said Sanders. Talbot Duckmanton, the assistant general manager of the ABC, refused to comment.

Planned performances at the University of New South Wales were also banned. The student group who tried to organise the two appearances was headed by Richard Neville, later to figure in his own obscenity trials in Australia and England. Neville, then editor of the student newspaper *Tharunka*, said the warden of the University Union cancelled Bruce's two shows in the Union cafeteria three hours after confirming the bookings in writing. He suspected 'arm-twisting' from above.

While all this was going on around him, Lenny Bruce invited another reporter, this time from the *Sunday Mirror*, into his hotel room. The unnamed journalist reported that Bruce paced the room 'like a jaguar with a toothache' as he explained his motivation.

''They call me obscene?' he wondered before producing a clipping from a Sydney newspaper. It showed an advertisement for the movie *Lolita*, featuring the famous image of the teenage American actress Sue Lyon wearing her heart-shaped sunglasses. He read out the film's slogan: 'Lock up your husbands … *Lolita* will be in Sydney in 15 days' time'. He seemed genuinely outraged by this. 'And they call me obscene! I don't get it.'

Lenny Bruce made one further public appearance in Sydney, playing a final show at the now defunct Wintergarten Theatre at Rose Bay. This grand old cinema had a capacity of 2000 but only between 50 and 200 (according to various reports) were now interested enough to pay to see him.

The promoter Lee Gordon lost a small fortune on the tour. Towards the end, defeated, he said: 'Lenny Bruce has accused me, by bringing him to Australia, of doing the equivalent of booking Hermann Goering to appear at a Jewish charity dance.'

# chapter **seventeen**

# **Toplessness**

**B**y 1964 it seemed that the tsunami created by Reard's bikini design was dissipating on the shores of Australia.

In the May 1964 issue of *Squire* magazine, 'the new magazine for modern men', a milestone of sorts was recorded.

'Historians will note the date—February 3—for it was the first day in the new year that the daily press managed to unearth a dissident voice on the subject which once had critics clamoring to be heard', declared a special *Squire* report on bikini-related matters.

That voice of dissent, curiously, came from one of Australia's more prominent bikini babes. It was over practical, not moral, matters. Tanya Binning, the then girlfriend of surfer Midget Farrelly, complained that riding a surfboard in a bikini caused tummy chafe.

*Squire* wondered if the bikini was now so well accepted that it was almost ignored?

Not when the top was removed.

According to the popular press, 1964 was the official birth of the topless swimsuit, or the 'kini' as some called it. Supposedly a global phenomenon, it could better be described as a series of co-ordinated publicity stunts. *Pix* magazine chronicled the fad in October 1964, suggesting that the pioneer was Lucki Winn, an exotic dancer who posed in a topless suit on Santa Monica beach while bemused policemen looked on from a patrol car. It was reported that girls not wearing tops were an increasingly common sight on the French Riviera.

By this stage Australia had already responded to the international challenge. The first recorded sighting of a topless swimsuit on a Sydney beach was Finnish model Tuija Pakerinen at Mona Vale in July 1964. Earlier that same month Sandra Nelson, a teenage Kings Cross stripper born in Russia, attracted even more attention when she conducted a tour of Sydney wearing a black topless dress.

Although Sandra described it as 'a dare', it was also a clever publicity stunt by the Pink Pussy Cat Club who had the foresight to arrange for a freelance photographer to accompany her.

Sandra's Topless Tour included The Rocks, George Street, The Sydney Harbour Bridge and, most memorably, a trip on the Manly Ferry where she was shown enjoying a toffee apple. It was a chilly winter's day so she wore an overcoat in between photo opportunities.

These snapshots appeared on the front page of the following day's tabloids, with her most prominent features hidden by black patches. The police did not charge her (there was no official complaint) but warned her not to do it again. She later apologised for the stunt on a television interview and promised she would never wear the dress again.

She changed her mind. Two weeks later she appeared at a lunchtime review at Sydney University wearing the dress plus two tassels over her nipples. Six hundred students paid to see her.

Some of the strongest criticism of Sandra's actions came from an unlikely source—her

A rare shot of Sandra Nelson with her top buttoned up.

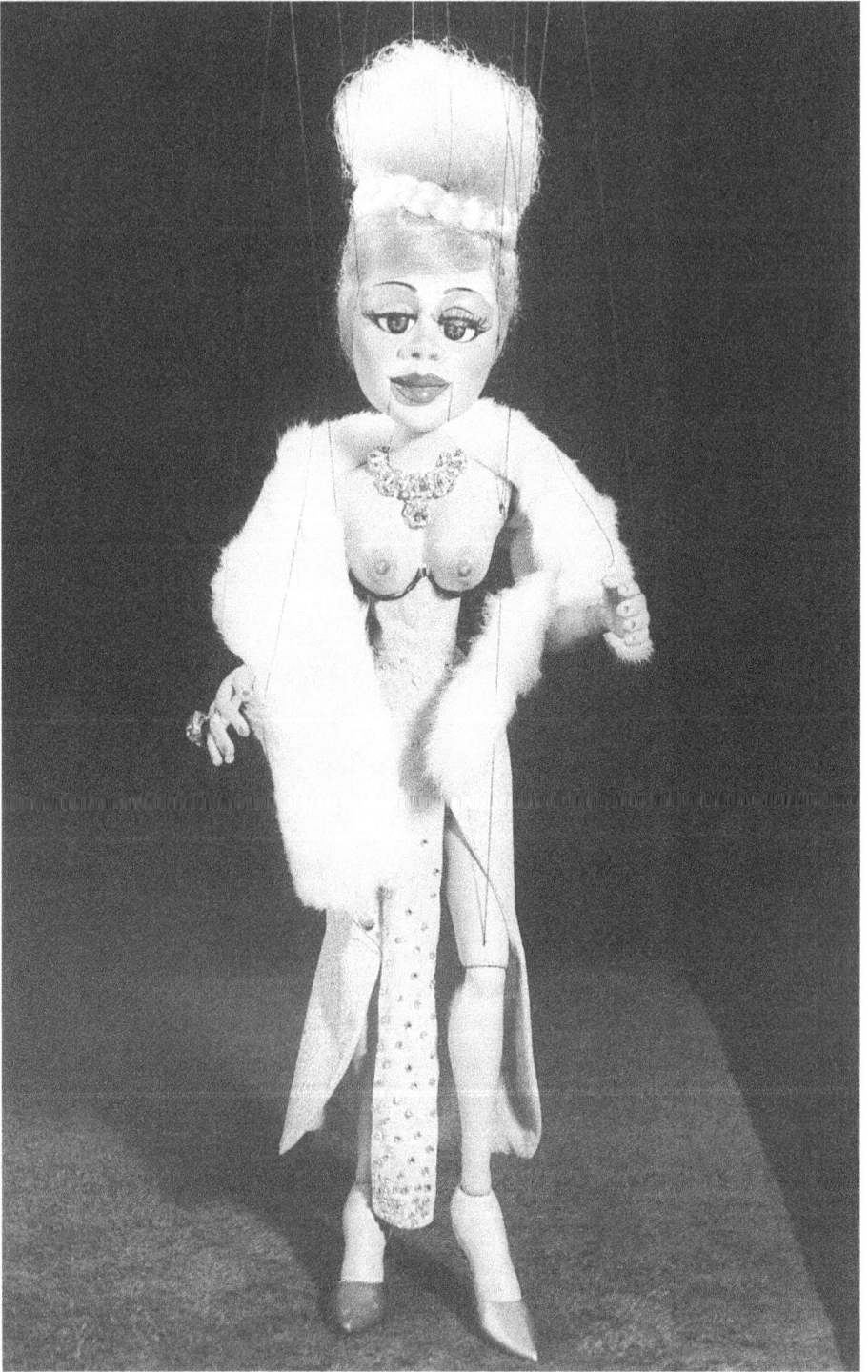

sisterhood of strippers. At the time, exotic dancers were still forced by law to wear those two small fabric discs—known as pasties in the trade—over their nipples when they worked. Now such outfits, even less, were being worn on the streets and the beaches. What the girls feared was that the topless craze would put them out of work.

'It all seems crazy', suggested one Kings Cross cop, quoted anonymously in *Pix*.

> 'A girl has to wear pasties in one of those strip places until she finishes work. Then she can take them off and walk out onto the street completely bare on top. Under the law we can do nothing unless somebody protests.'

Sandra Nelson exploited this legal loophole enthusiastically, being paid huge amounts of money to simply turn up at functions and mingle with the guests wearing the infamous Manly Ferry dress. She was occasionally charged, most notably at Windsor after she had made an appearance as a trophy girl at a speedway meeting. Later that day she was seen walking down the main street with her bra in one hand and her shirt in the other. She told the court that someone had dared her to take off her top so she did. She was fined six pounds.

'She does not mean any malice, or to offend people, and she is a clean, decent girl, permanently employed', said her lawyer in her defence.

Permanently employed, thanks to her publicity stunts, as Australia's best paid stripper. Such was her popularity that The Bergs, a puppet troupe, introduced a Sandra 'Topless' Nelson marionette.

Her role in the sexual revolution seems to have been largely ignored, at least when compared to events like the *Oz* trial which took place at around the same time. Much later when I met up with

OPPOSITE: In 1964 even puppets went topless.

'Topless suits' were advertised, but only for use in 'private pools'.

Sandra, these days using her original Russian name and living in America, she explained that she was partly motivated by a need for money (she had just run away from a migrant camp in Wollongong), but also by a desire to challenge the social rules that said girls weren't allowed to do such things.

For women who weren't exotic dancers, the 1964 topless fad made little impact. Special topless swimsuits (it wasn't enough to just throw away the top of a bikini) were advertised in local magazines … 'for private use only'. The majority of women were not yet ready to wear these in public although the more daring tried see-through tops. It would take another 15 years or so for bikini tops to start dropping like flies, but the idea was controversial enough.

In a 1964 interview, Dulcie Deamer, the Queen of Bohemia in the Roaring Twenties, said she deplored the topless craze.

'As I see it, the question is not one of morality but of aesthetics', she commented. 'I've been a nudist all my life but I wouldn't wear one of these things. They're inartistic.'

The topless fad supplied *Pix* and *Australasian Post* with a range of headlines for several months and kept the moral guardians on red alert for years. There were even reports of toplessness invading that most unlikely of locations, Canberra. In July, the chilliest of months, the recently launched *Australian* newspaper tried to boost its meagre circulation by running a hopeful report that at least one local woman, 'blonde, attractive and in her early 20s' had walked into a shop in Civic and asked to buy a topless dress.

According to the manager, 'she told me she'd tried everywhere, and was going to keep trying until she got the dress she wanted'. The fashion controller of a Canberra department store added that he had planned to have a model parade the new style, but there had been such uproar over a similar proposal in Newcastle, that he had decided against it.

Also reported was a rumour that a girl would be making an appearance in a topless frock in Monaro Mall during late shopping on Friday night. Canberra detectives were there just in case. They said that if seen, she would have been charged with offensive behaviour.

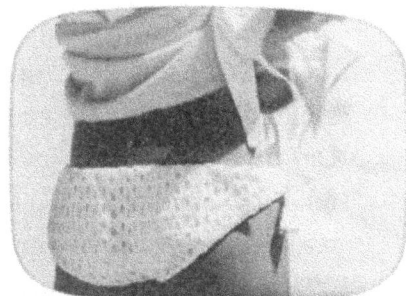

Sea & Ski tanning lotion exploited the growing topless craze in this 1968 television commercial.

A precursor to this fad happened in Sydney in 1960 when two mermaid sculptures were placed on Ben Buckler, the large rock that marks the northern extreme of Bondi Beach.

The mermaids were made of fibreglass and fibro cement and painted gold, modelled from life by sculptor Lyall Randolph, the so-called 'Leonardo da Vinci of Bondi'. Two local beach beauties, Jan Carmody, Miss Australian Surf 1959, and Lyn Whillier, a Commonwealth Games breaststroker, posed for Randolph. Both girls insisted that they had worn bikini tops in the studio, but when the mermaids appeared on top of the rock, they were naked from the waist up and anatomically accurate enough to provoke the wonderfully named Dr Rumble, a spokesperson for the Catholic Church. He issued the following statement: 'We can hardly complain if young men, their passions inflamed, commit sex offences'.

It was common for pranksters to climb the rock and place bras on the mermaids. One was washed off the rock in 1979, around the time that real-life topless women began invading Bondi. If you want to see what so inflamed Dr Rumble, the remains of the second mermaid are now placed in a tamper-proof glass case in Waverley Library.

Tops stayed on, but by the late 1960s, there were indications of a gradual loosening of straps. The more adventurous sunbathers began by unclipping the back strap while lying flat on their stomachs, sliding off the shoulder straps one by one, then, sometime around 1975, slipping the top off and rolling onto their backs.

The timing of this final moment of toplessness depended on where you lived. Sydney was the first to accept the inevitable. One of the last recorded topless arrests in Sydney was made in September 1975 on Harbord Beach when one woman, among a group of three women and three men, was charged with offensive behaviour by three Manly detectives.

Called to the crime scene, the cops noticed that all three women were sunbathing topless but only one was arrested because she was lying on her back when the detectives arrived. The two women lying on their stomachs were not deemed offensive.

The law regarding offensive behaviour stated that police action could only be taken if there was a complaint made. While police were still likely to act on a complaint against a totally nude person, by 1978 they had clearly given up trying to keep the tops on bikinis.

'If we arrested every topless woman sunbather we wouldn't have room in the courts', said one Northern Beaches police officer quoted anonymously in the *Sun-Herald*. 'Topless bathing is becoming just taken for granted and most women pick mainly isolated areas.'

As further proof of this general acceptance, by 1977, photos of topless women were regularly appearing in that bastion of middle-class conservatism, the *Australian Women's Weekly*. Not in the editorial section (our Ita wouldn't have allowed that) but in full-page, full-colour ads for the Philips Ultraphil Sun Lamp, under the headline 'They're going to love your body on the beach this summer'. The message is obvious. If you're going to bare your breasts on the beach this summer, you should tan them in advance.

In the same issue of the magazine, naked, fully tanned women were also shown in ads for Piz Buin tanning lotion and Depilatron hair removal—two essential accessories for the modern sun worshipper.

It's worth pointing out that this was just over ten years since bare breasts had first started to appear in magazines like *Man*. Now nipples had invaded the offices of the *Australian Women's Weekly*.

The tide had officially turned. In the summer of 1978/1979 the southern half of Bondi was made legally topless, despite official protest from church groups.

Father James O'Reilly, a local Catholic priest, led the campaign. He delivered a fiery sermon in which he described the topless trend as a 'swelling and running sore'.

# chapter **eighteen**
# Much ado about nothing

'The nudist season is due for a gala opening this month', reported the *Australasian Post* in September 1952. 'Nudists are already outgrowing their colonies in New South Wales. Hundreds more are expected to join the suntan-all-over brigade this summer.'

Despite the dire warnings of 'Atlantis' in 1935 … 'as for mixed nudism—well, whoever started that idea needs a medical examination' … mixed nudism was thriving just after the First World War.

Ron Ashworth, President of the Australasian Sunbathing Association, was Australia's King of Nudism. His association had 2000 members and at one stage ran four camps—one in the Blue Mountains and three in the outer suburbs of Sydney. He credited the popularity of the activity with the increase in post-war migration. In 1952, Ashworth announced plans to establish a much larger colony on an island near Jervis Bay on the New South Wales' South Coast, transport being provided by flying-boat.

'Australians are now more enlightened about nudism', said Ashworth. 'People no longer regard nudists as a bunch of cranks who want to run around without their clothes.'

Ashworth had been a naturist for 20 years and was now the publisher of several nudist publications, including *The Australian Sunbather, Nude Life in Australia, Naturism Illustrated* and *Maids of Australia*. Another Australian publication, *Health and Sunshine*, was also available.

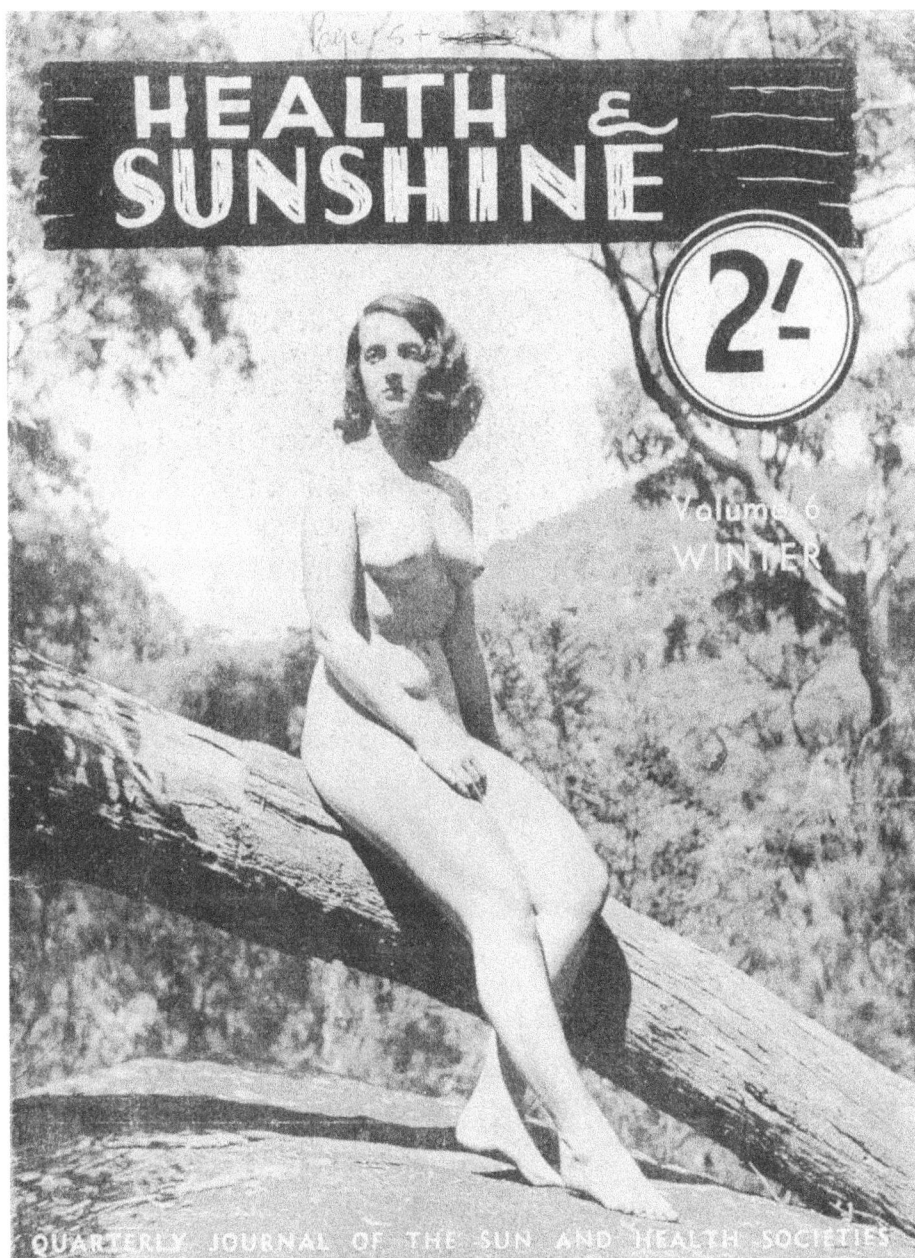

HEALTH & SUNSHINE

2/-

Volume 6
WINTER

QUARTERLY JOURNAL OF THE SUN AND HEALTH SOCIETIES

These magazines were controversial in that a naked figure, always a young woman, graced the cover at a time when no other magazine was allowed to show even partial nudity. About 90 per cent of the photos inside were of attractive women. Sales of the

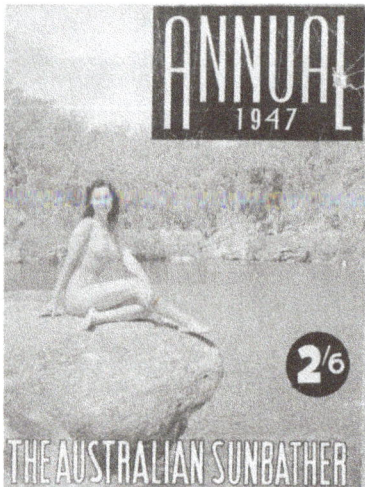

ABOVE: Series of nudist magazines in the 1940s.

'nudie' magazines, either under the counter in bookstalls or by subscription, were suspiciously greater than the number of active nudists. One clergyman said that *Australian Sunbather* magazine was an evil publication in that 'it pandered to impure sex instincts and was calculated to influence adolescents'. This comment was based partly on a Melbourne incident in which three small boys were found selling copies of *Australian Sunbather* on the steps of a hotel, promoting it to patrons as 'a sex book for a bob'.

A court case followed in which the magistrate decided that none of the naturist magazines produced in court unduly emphasised sex and dismissed the charge.

Ashworth defended his publications by pointing out that the models featured did not only always portray the ideal form as glamour girl magazines did. 'They reveal the hips and "bow windows", scrawny shoulders and skinny shanks which most people when they think about it must realise are concealed by men's and women's apparel.' The magazine's credo began with the phrase: 'We believe in the essential wholesomeness of the human body and all its functions.'

Ashworth said he regretted that, according to the law, he was forced to use the retoucher's airbrush to disguise the pubic area.

He admitted using a magnifying glass to make sure no stray pubic hairs were exposed. This was against the spirit of nudism in that partial nudity is considered more obscene than full exposure. He added that the true naturist always made a careful distinction between decent and indecent poses, although this probably escaped the critical facilities of a typical schoolboy behind the shelter shed.

*Australasian Post* gave a brief review of the contents of *Australian Sunbather.*

'Inside it is embellished with many other nude studies and snapshots of varying degrees of attractiveness, with notes from naturist organisations, health and diet advice (some supplied by the NSW Department of Public Health).' A 'Sunbathing Penfriends' section was included, with the majority of advertisements from men. A sample from August 1949: 'Truck driver, 24, single, would like to contact naturist of opposite sex, view to joining club. Interests are surfing, cars, photography. Write R.H., c/o this Journal.'

The entrepreneurial Ashworth also advertised a confidential photo developing service—'only genuine outdoor naturist pictures will be entertained, as we do not tolerate other types of nudist photography'—a home portraiture service and the opportunity to buy original studies. A range of publications imported from England were also available, including *Desiree,* a collection of nude studies of 'the loveliest girl in England', *Eternal Eve, Cavalcade of Beauty* and *Curves and Colour.* Some of these appeared to be on the borderline between art studies and cheesecake. *Ideal Manhood* was available for beefcake enthusiasts.

Just as some figured that these magazines were just an excuse to show naked women, there were those who assumed that there must be, as *Australasian Post* quaintly put it, 'goings on among groups of people of mixed sexes who gather and gambol in the nude—that the sight of the naked bodies of the opposite sex must engender erotic feelings and thus lead to immorality'.

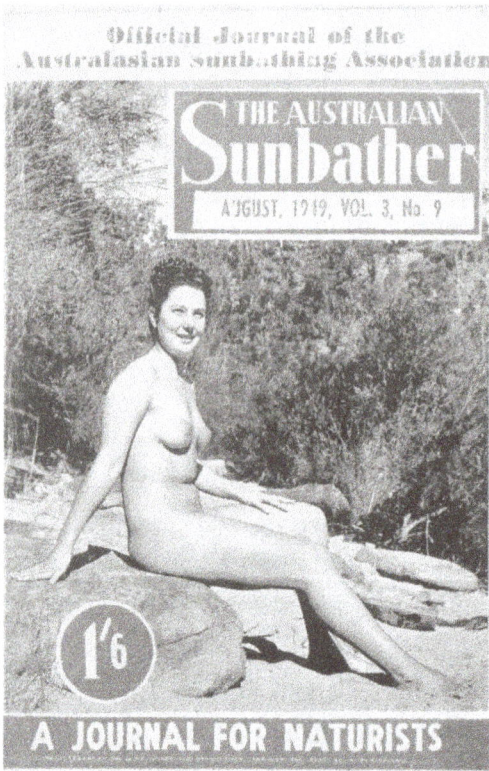

Official Journal of the
Australasian sunbathing Association

THE AUSTRALIAN
Sunbather
AUGUST, 1949, VOL. 3, No. 9

1'6

A JOURNAL FOR NATURISTS

At a time when magazine covers were closely monitored, naturist magazines revealed all.

Ashworth denied this, stating that social group nakedness places no emphasis whatever on sex. Members of his clubs caught 'canoodling, pairing-off or going away by themselves', were asked to resign.

As for the law, Ashworth said there were none in any Australian state forbidding nudism as such. Laws against 'lewd, lascivious, obscene and indecent' conduct did not apply to naturism unless it related to the 'in the presence of persons offended thereby' clause. This was unlikely because most colonies were restricted to members and situated on private properties.

After a Sunday newspaper had run a story on one of the first Sydney camps in bushland near Frenchs Forest, the Commissioner of Police announced that investigations would be made with a view to prosecution. Ashworth responded: 'We are in absolute seclusion so there is no nuisance to anybody. With all due respect to his office, I would not hesitate to ask the commissioner to join us, that is how sure I am.'

This kindly offer was declined.

Police did comb the bush looking for the secluded camp, but when they found it they were satisfied that it was properly organised, and made no charges.

There was an occasional problem with Peeping Toms (even the odd Peeping Thomasina) especially at the Woodlands Camp near

Liverpool, which sat close to Bankstown Airport. In 1950, three members of the Royal Aero Club were suspended by the NSW Regional Director of Civil Aviation after being spotted flying low over the camp.

'We complained about airmen flying low, not because we disliked their attention, but because we thought we might take their attention off the flying and they would crash', said Frank Thomas, the Woodlands manager, who later suggested that in 20 years time no one would be bothered by the sight of naked bodies and we'd be able to tolerate mixed nude bathing on local beaches.

He was right and he was wrong.

By the early 1970s there were well-known nude beaches in most states, unofficially so until Don Dunstan, our swingingest premier, gave his political stamp of approval to Maslin Beach, 50 kilometres south of Adelaide.

Australia's first legal weekend of skinny-dipping on a public beach took place in February 1975 when a few hundred genuine nudists—identified by their all-over tans and air of nonchalance—were outnumbered by hordes of fully-clothed observers, some sweating it out in parked cars with binoculars.

'Among the clothed perverts here today are more than 100 bikies and the character of the beach has changed overnight', complained Mrs Wyn Pettifor, a JP and mother of seven, who fronted a local protest group.

Victorian Premier, Rupert Hamer, responded to Dunstan's initiative by saying, 'I don't go into it myself but I think it's worth looking at.' Pun intended.

In Sydney throughout the early 1970s nudists had gathered, unofficially, at Lady Jane Beach. Also known as Lady Bay, this delightful sheltered cove is at the end of a bush track near the tip of South Head. There is a six-metre sheer drop from the cliffs to the sand. In those days the only means of access was by two rickety ladders, or by small boat.

Its unique geography made it ideal for nude bathing but also ideal for police raids, and they attacked in force during the summer of 1974/1975.

Access to the beach was by rickety ladders, or boats. The nudies were trapped.

These raids were planned with all the precision of a military invasion. The strategy went something like this. A police vanguard, wearing plain-cossies, arrived at the beach by unmarked speedboat. They mingled with the crowd as inconspicuously as is possible for anyone wearing clothing to mingle with those who aren't. Meanwhile a back-up squad, in standard-issue grey police overalls, was positioned at the top of the cliffs. The nudies were trapped.

On one hot Friday afternoon in December 1974, 42

people were arrested by a team of police which included 'women constables in bikinis' according to Sydney's *Daily Sun* newspaper. Those arrested were ordered to regain their modesty before being ordered up the ladders and then escorted to waiting trucks. They were taken to the nearest cop shop and charged with indecent exposure.

Some of the nudists tried to swim for it, others attempted to escape by scrambling over rocks. Tanya Hall, a 20-year-old on holiday from Melbourne, told a newspaper reporter she had hidden naked in a bush while the raid was taking place.

'It was the most disgusting infringement of human rights I have seen', she said. 'Everyone was treated as if they were dangerous criminals instead of citizens.'

To add to the air of confusion, a number of women wearing bikini bottoms were also arrested. Perhaps they would only be given half the sentence? Of those arrested 25 did not bother to turn up at court, forfeiting bail of $20.

The first raid by the police special task force—soon to be dubbed the Peep Squad by the media—had the exact opposite effect to what was intended.

'Sydney's nude bathers defied police yesterday by taking to the sun in even bigger numbers', reported the *Sun* newspaper the following Monday. 'There were more than ever at their favourite haunt … and there were other naked sunbathers at several other small beaches around the harbour.'

Lady Jane, the following weekend, was virtually standing room only. The large crowd of sunlovers was joined by an audience of a hundred or so clothed spectators occupying the rock ledges overlooking the beach. The nudists were prepared. They appointed lookouts—cockatoos according to criminal slang—to signal the arrival of police.

It was all faintly ludicrous at a time when nude bodies were openly displayed on prime-time TV shows like 'Number 96' and

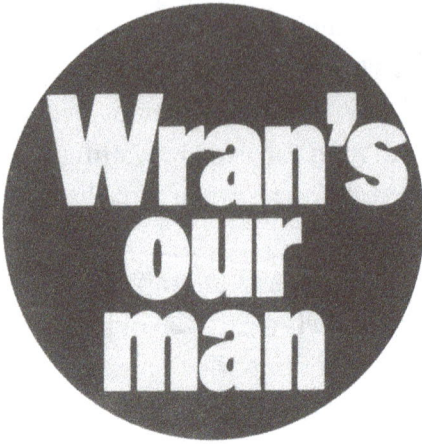

Neville's campaign slogan clearly showed who was boss.

'The Box'. The movie based on the latter series was promoted by three models parading through the lunchtime streets of Sydney wearing only the bottom halves of bikinis, cork-heeled platform shoes, and small placards around their waists saying 'It All Comes Off On "The Box"'.

'Certainly some people are offended by the sight of nude bodies on the sand', suggested the *Sunday Telegraph* in a typical editorial. 'But more people are offended by Sydney's staggering crime rate. The police force—which spends only about 20 per cent of its time investigating crime—should stop being silly.'

Further raids were made during the summer, some sillier than others. On one occasion in February, two men and one woman were chosen at random and taken away by officers in a rubber duckie while, according to one eyewitness, another 60 or 70 naked persons stood around watching and laughing.

The entire episode was a public relations disaster for Police Minister John Waddy and Police Commisioner Fred Hanson. Waddy even admitted in NSW Parliament that he and Hanson had made a secret visit to Lady Jane beach in January, adding that yes, he had definitely seen naked bodies on that occasion. Roars of laughter came from the opposition's benches.

Neville Wran, the then Leader of the Opposition, made the most of this golden political opportunity, describing the actions of Waddy and Hanson as farcical and promising to establish two legal nude beaches if he was elected.

Voters obviously approved. By the summer of 1976/1977, Wran had been elected NSW Premier. His liberal approach to nudity helped create an image as a swinging, seventies kind of guy.

On Saturday 24 October, 1976, he kept his election promise.

The people of Sydney were now free to go naked at two public beaches—Lady Jane and Reef Beach near Balgowlah—without fear of being grabbed by cops in rubber duckies. The Peep Squad was disbanded but one burning question remains. With detectives wearing Speedos and woman constables disguised in brief bikinis, where did those intrepid officers keep their badges? A police media spokesperson was unable to provide me with an answer.

Once nudity was made legal there were predictable complaints from locals, especially at Reef Beach, where angry residents pointed out that some nudists were walking back to their cars before bothering to get dressed.

The most memorable protest came from television sportscaster Rex Mossop, better known as The Moose or Sexy Rexy, who lived in Beatty Street, the closest parking point to the beach. His was a very physical form of censorship. In November, Mossop made a citizen's arrest of a man walking naked past his house.

'He was already in his car desperately trying to pull on his trousers by the time I got to him', said Mossop. 'I asked him if he would walk nude down his own suburban street in front of his wife or mother-in-law or the neighbours and he said of course he wouldn't.'

The citizen's arrest was made under sub-section 1 of Section 352 of the Crimes Act, which authorises anyone, under certain circumstances, to apprehend another during or immediately after a suspected offence. Citizen's arrests are rarely made and not recommended by police unless, as in Mossop's case, you are a former international rugby league representative noted for your tackling skills.

The incident is best-remembered these days for inspiring perhaps the best of Mossop's many notable quotes. He is alleged to have said to reporters: 'I don't see why we should have male genitals thrust down our throat.'

Although not against nudism in principle (he confessed he liked to get naked on his sun lounge in the privacy of his own backyard), Mossop remained a staunch critic of nudism on Reef Beach where he had swum since 1938. Among his complaints was the claim that 'there have been indecent acts committed on the beach and local children have been approached and sometimes chased by these people'.

There were problems of a different kind on the south side of the harbour. In March 1977, some anonymous critic with a saw sabotaged one of the now infamous Lady Jane ladders, removing every second rung.

After a six-month trial, Premier Wran declared the experiment a success.

# chapter **nineteen**
# **Naughty little boys**

**J**ust as films featuring 'prolonged embraces' were to blame for moral decay in the 1940s, and comic books were the culprits in the 1950s, in the 1960s it was girlie magazines, according to *A Guide to Manhood*.

If you were a teenager growing up in the 1960s, chances are you would have been handed a copy of *A Guide to Manhood* as soon as your voice broke. Promoting itself as 'a reliable graded sex education booklet for young men 15 years and over', it was published locally by Professor Harvey Sutton OBE of the Father and Son Welfare Movement. A separate mother and daughter section produced similar books for girls.

The popularity of these sex education manuals was significant. Around 240 000 copies of *A Guide to Manhood* had been published by the time the third, revised edition was released in 1961. At the start of the decade that ended with Woodstock, the advice given seems almost Edwardian.

Masturbation is discussed but not recommended—'a rather immature form of sex expression'—and homosexuality is seen as both unnatural and an impediment to a future happy marriage—'the lad who becomes a partner in activities of this nature is turning the sex instinct in an entirely wrong direction'.

The most strongly worded warning concerns dirty books and magazines.

'On many bookstore counters today can be found numerous publications which have as their main attraction suggestive stories and pictures concerning sex. The damaging effect these publications have on the mind of a person can be very considerable. They present sex in an entirely wrong light and they hold up the noble relationship of a man and a woman as a thing of ridicule and shame. They present the relationship on the basis of lust rather than deep, enduring love and consideration of each other.'

As proof of the dangers of such lustful publications, the booklet provides details of an incident in which an unnamed 16-year-old boy had committed a 'grievous sexual assault' on his 14-year-old sister. Looking for a motive, their mother had found a pile of such magazines hidden at the bottom of her son's wardrobe.

'He had filled his mind on this material until it so dominated his thinking, so warped his outlook, that it drove him to that very tragic offence', suggests the booklet.

Man magazine produced this curiously named Junior edition.

The exact nature and titles of these magazines is not mentioned, but my personal research into the contents of early 1960s bookstalls suggests that *Man* magazine or *Gals and Gags* would have been the most likely culprits. There was little else openly available at the time that could be called suggestive. *Gals and Gags*, featuring babes in bikinis and RSL humour that wouldn't raise an eyebrow these days, was considered wicked enough to be banned in Queensland. But then, just about everything was banned in Queensland, especially early imported issues of *Playboy*.

One of several attempts to have the thoughts of Chairman Hugh Hefner available to Queensland swingers was made in 1963 by the HMH Publishing Co. Inc. of Chicago. The proposal was stonewalled by Mr A. Bennett of the State Literature Board of Review who said the magazine openly advocated licentiousness and pre-marital relations.

*Man* magazine, which first started in Australia in 1935, also had literary pretensions, sandwiching their pin-up pages between pseudo-sophisticated articles, action-packed short stories and sporting profiles. For those who only wanted to perve, the publishers produced a spin-off, minus the informative articles, aimed directly at the smutty little boy market. It was quaintly called *Man Junior*.

In my experience, *Man Junior* was the magazine most likely to be passed around the toilet blocks at my own alma mater, Glenelg Primary School.

It was pretty tame stuff, even by the mild standards of the day, and some were already thinking about producing their own harder-edged smut. In 1962, three entrepreneurial Perth boys were charged with selling a series of obscene photos at three school-yards. The trio had organised a model, taken the shots, had them developed and printed, then arranged healthy sales and distribu-tion (at 2 shillings a photo) at three schoolyards.

'You are a dirty-minded collection of lads', said special magis-trate Arney in Perth Children's Court. The three boys were all aged 14. Their apparently willing model was 12.

*Oz* magazine was launched on April Fool's Day, 1963, by three young men not much older than the aforementioned Perth entre-preneurs. Richard Walsh, Richard Neville and Martin Sharp were all at various Sydney universities, recent graduates from some of Syd-ney's most exclusive private schools. Their magazine, largely self-funded, made an instant impact. The first issue of *Oz* sparked a charge of obscenity. Two of the three editors pleaded guilty and

Methodist minister Reverend Roger Bush has been seen lately on Sydney's northern beaches armed with a tape-recorder to conduct his own sociological survey of teenagers' habits, morals, etc. Oz reproduces below a replica of a fairly typical conversation anyone can overhear at the Newport Arms Hotel (nerve-centre of the party-crashing clique) on any Saturday night. It's not the sort of thing Reverend Bush will be playing to his ABC listening audience; however, **if you read this aloud in a guttural, awkwardly emphatic monotone, then you will enjoy a more accurate understanding of our beach boys' habits than a hundred ABC programmes could supply.**

COURTESY OF MARTIN SHARP

The word flashed round the Arms that there was a GAS turn up at Whale Beach Rd, so we piled into the Mini Coopers and thrashed over and y'know what the old man of the bird who was having the turn said we couldn't crash — so Dennis belted him and we all piled in and there was a helluva lot of grog and plus th' tin tubes the fellers brought up from the Arms, we all managed to get pretty pissed — there were a few KING birds there but they were holding hands with these fairies — so DENNIS belted them and we all got onto the birds and Frank got one of them so pissed that she passed out so we all dragged her out to the garage and went through her like a packet of salts — KING! Then the old lady of the bird who was having the turn said she'd ring the Johns so Sid chucked all over her and she got hysterical and then Phil did this so Dennis BELTED her and then Phil did this and ran King hambone on the kitchen table and ran round the house in the raw ripping the gear off all the birds — God yes KING! and then this little dingo crap told Phil to leave his bird alone so Phil got Dennis and Dennis SMASHED him — God Dennis is baking lighter, irritating to take — he really is and it really was a GAS turn and I had a KING time and Sid whose the funniest bloke I know ralphed in the T.V. set and chucked in it and it was FUNNY.....

You be the judge. This Oz magazine satire on 1960s' surfie culture was deemed obscene in 1964.

paid a fine of 20 pounds each. It was the best publicity campaign any magazine could have. Within a year *Oz* circulation had reached 40 000, a staggering amount for an independent magazine. By the end of the year it was available in Melbourne, Adelaide and Canberra as well as Sydney. Posters asking, 'Will this deprave, corrupt you?' were put up outside newsagencies.

They now knew they were onto a good thing and began to see how far they could go by sending up politics, religion, high society and even the current fad for Beatlemania. Nothing was sacred.

Then things got nasty. A Vice Squad detective picked up a copy of *Oz* No. 6, which hit the news stands in February 1964. The cop was initially offended by the cover showing three young men (the editors, according to one theory) appearing to piss into the modernist sculpted fountain on the side of the P&O Building in Hunter Street, Sydney.

'To alleviate the severe drabness of its sandstone façade', ran the cover text, 'sculptor Tom Bass has set an attractive bronze urinal in the wall for the convenience of passers-by.'

Once he looked inside, the detective was also not amused by words or drawings on pages 4, 5, 6, 7, 13 and 16 (note, the magazine was only 16 pages). Among the more offensive bits were a

After the trial, the *Oz* team continued to push the boundaries.

cartoon on page 4 and a satire of Northern Beaches surfie culture on page 7, both written and drawn by Martin Sharp. This time there would be no slap on the wrist.

IN THE GARDEN
## CARDINUS GILROYUS
By WARATAH

Choose a luxurious home for this ancient flower to display its finery. The Gilroyus is a prolific bloomer and makes a magnificent display en masse. However to thrive it requires complete dedication since it must have rich and constant attention. The Gilroyus comes from an old Roman strain which is

said to have no roots. The original of the species — Cardinus Magdalena Virgo — is believed to have been self-pollinating. This quality has now been lost, but the species retains an extraordinary sensitivity to interference in the breeding process. Flowers are a deep bluey colour and reach their finest show around Easter time. All specimens of this genus require frequent applications of bull manure.

### ON THE PROWL

Thank you, dear OZ, for publishing that poignant memoir of a prowler in the last issue. May I add something?

You see, I used to be a prowler too. A female prowler. I loved to stare at men undressing. But no one ever took me seriously. I didn't proposition a single soul ... no indignant householder attacked me ... there was no publicity.

Often when I was on the prowl the police cars pulled up and the officers insisted on escorting me home — to save me from the prowler. Once I longed to see those friendly Detective sergeants in the raw.

I finally kicked the prowling habit after I met my boy-friend. I shall never forget our first meeting. This young couple were stripping off, and I was gazing at the husband when I suddenly spied HIM on the other side of the roadway. He was staring at the wife.

We're been going steady ever since. We strip off and just stare at each other. No sex. We just stare.

### READY FOR A DAY IN BED

"I'm not too bad for an old man," the Prime Minister, Sir Robert Menzies told reporters at Kingsford Smith airport yesterday.

THE SUN-HERALD, JULY 19, 1964

OZ AUGUST Page 12

The three editors were charged with publishing an obscene publication under the Obscene and Indecent Publications Act of 1955. The act defined obscene as 'unduly emphasising matters of sex, crimes of violence, gross cruelty or horror'—a description that had previously applied to trashy American detective novels, comics and 'true crime' magazines. At the same time as it was applied to *Oz*, the Act was also being invoked to prevent *Cavalier*, an American 'man interest magazine', from being distributed here.

Also charged over *Oz* was Francis James, accused of having printed the magazine. There was some irony in this as James was also honorary managing director of the Anglican Press. His main job was the editing and publishing of *The Anglican* magazine.

The trial began in September in the Central Court of Petty Sessions. Newspaper reports made the front pages, in part because of the high calibre of legal talent recruited. Eight university academics, four art and drama critics, two psychiatrists and Miss Betty Archdale, headmistress of Abbotsleigh Girls' College, were among those appearing as witnesses for the defence. John Kerr and Neville Wran, later to become famous in their own rights, appeared to debate the principles of free speech. Their argument was based largely on Section 3 (3) of the Act, which states in part:

'In determining for the purposes of the Act whether any publication or advertisement is obscene the court shall have regard to—(a) the nature of the publication or advertisement and (b) the persons, classes of persons and age groups to or amongst whom the publications or advertisements was or was intended or likely to be published etc.'

Also crucial to the defence was Section 4, which excludes from prosecution 'any work of literary or artistic merit'. But, in terms of the Act, the Court alone would decide if there was any 'undue emphasis on sex'. That decision would be made by Gerry Locke, SM, a man not noted for his sense of humour.

This was serious stuff which saw some of the great legal minds of that generation arguing the obscenity, or not, of the words 'Get Folked'.

Adding a further comic touch to proceedings, Walsh, Neville and Sharp appeared in court wearing their old school uniforms. In hindsight, Neville said this was a tactic suggested by their lawyer that probably worked against them. They were lambs in the slaughterhouse.

'This room smells of death', commented Martin Sharp during the proceedings. 'It smells as though the air's been locked up here for centuries with none but old men to breathe it.'

It had been a fraught period for Sharp. In August he had also been one of four charged over an article published in the University of New South Wales student newspaper, *Tharunka*. The students were found guilty and fined under the Obscene and Indecent Publications Act, but all appealed successfully.

Considering his verdict in the *Oz* trial, Locke SM, said that this magazine contained articles which were filthy, disgusting, offensive, libellous and blasphemous. He rejected the evidence of academics who had said that the material was unlikely to deprave, reserving special scorn for Professor Stout, head of philosophy at the University of Sydney, who had claimed: 'I do not know what an obscene word is. Four letter words never corrupted anyone.'

'This room smells of death'; Martin Sharp in his old Cranbrook uniform.

Locke rejected that. 'Such evidence runs contrary to life and is an insult to the intelligence of the court. No reasonable person doubts that depravity corrupts just as no person doubts indiscriminate use of four-letter words is likely to deprave.'

He said that it was also reasonable to assume that the magazine would probably get into the hands of adolescents or immature and unhealthy-minded adults.

The magistrate then assessed the defence of literary merit. 'With considerable doubt and hesitation I feel bound to hold in law the magazine does have literary and artistic merit. Smut with humour is the literary device of the gutter and smut remains smut even when satire is used as its vehicle.'

Then, in summing up. 'It is high time the publication of this type of magazine was stopped.'

He attempted to do so by giving the three editors the maximum possible sentence. Richard Neville and Richard Walsh received six-month sentences while Martin Sharp got four months. Oz Publications was fined 100 pounds while Francis James of *The Anglican* received a 50-pound fine. All appealed their sentences and the three sentenced to prison were released on bail.

The severity of the verdict shocked even the general public who had never heard of *Oz* magazine. When the appeal was finally heard a year and seven months after the Vice Squad detective had picked up a copy and been offended, Judge Levine of the Quarter Sessions Appeal Court determined that the publication was not obscene and had not duly emphasised sex. He was the same judge who had overturned the *Tharunka* convictions.

'I repeat what I said in the *Tharunka* case: "We are living in times when great freedom of expression in matters of sex is accepted by the community".'

In his view, neither publication infringed the standard of the community of the whole. Within 19 months Neville, Walsh and Sharp had gone from being branded peddlers of smut to being the pioneers of new community sexual standards. This verdict would inspire the social changes that would influence the entire decade.

*Oz* magazine continued to be published until 1968, two years after Neville and Sharp moved to England to produce a separate version which also confronted the British legal system. Meanwhile, in Australia, a new permissive period in publishing was beginning. What would have been considered obscene ten years ago was now being sold openly on street corners.

'Bawdy, comic, scurrilous, irreverent, occasionally satirical and often immature', was Gordon Chancellor's description of the Kings Cross *Whisper* nearly a quarter of a century after he had been involved in its creation. The *Whisper* remains a publishing landmark, if not for its content then for its astonishing success. The satirical newspaper was founded on New Year's Day, 1965, by journalists Terry Blake and Jim Ramsay, inspired by the popularity of a similar newspaper that Ramsay had launched in Darwin—the *Waratah Whisper*. The mix of spoof stories and photos of bare-breasted ladies had gone down well at football club nights and in pubs and Blake and Ramsay decided that a similar publication should be equally popular if sold around Kings Cross on New Year's Eve.

According to legend, they had to hock everything they owned, and a few things they didn't, to raise the printing costs. And when it was printed (12 tabloid pages) they had to sell it themselves, standing on street corners with a bundle in one arm. 'Get your *Whisper* before it's banned' was one of their catch cries.

A strange thing happened. By early morning the word had spread so quickly around Sydney that people were heading in from the outer suburbs in cars in the hope of picking up a copy. By dawn Blake and Ramsay realised they were on a winner. In one night the newspaper that was only ever planned as a one-off had established

The 'adults only' adventures of Martha Hurry, as drawn by Fred Cullen, were a feature of the Kings Cross *Whisper*.

a word-of-mouth reputation that enabled it to be printed on a regular basis and sold through a network of independent street sellers recruited from the Kings Cross underground.

'They were coming from everywhere. Word had spread through the brokers, the push, the pub hustlers, the no-hopers, the basket cases and all manner of unemployed artists, musos, actors, writers, etc.', recalled Terry Blake in 1988.

'Here was an easy quid and no strings attached. Without warning, the city of Sydney was swarming with unwashed hippies and their bedraggled girlfriends thrusting rude newspapers into the startled faces of peak hour commuters. From Palm Beach to Liverpool, a plague was upon the land and there didn't seem to be anything anyone could do about it. There was nothing illegal about selling papers on street corners and as long as the owners didn't object, the same went for pubs and other temples of urban worship.'

There was, however, something illegal about selling obscenity. The *Whisper* stopped short of the line that the publishers of *Oz* had unwittingly stepped over or, more likely, the courts were now less enthusiastic about policing moral matters. The *Whisper*'s sense of satire was less political than *Oz*, aimed more at the IQ of the average bloke down the pub. The cartoons and photos of naked women were no more explicit than what you might find in magazines freely available in the darker corners of newsagencies. Pubic hairs were not shown. What made this newspaper sell was its larrikin appeal. It was anti-authority but in an old-fashioned way, like betting with an SP bookie.

Blake and Ramsay printed 25 000 copies of their second edition. These sold out in one day and the second print run of 20 000 also sold out. A year later they were printing 150 000 copies, sold by a network of around 200 street vendors, some of whom became identities in their own right.

There was Tom the Throat, Laugh-a-lot Langley, The Lone Ranger and Milo, the latter securing the prime position on the corner of Darlinghurst and Bayswater roads in the heart of the Cross. Uncle Sam, with a goatee beard and a Stars and Stripes waistcoat, was a regular at Town Hall Station, pointing at commuters and saying, 'Your *Whisper* needs you'. Brian 'Stark' Raven, who went on to form the Australian Nazi Party, and Geoffrey Chandler of Bogle-Chandler fame, were *Whisper* sellers based in Balmain.

The publication had its detractors. Newspapers, television and radio took the expected conservative line, describing the paper as 'a truly filthy publication' that 'wallowed in schoolboy jokes and lavatory humour'—two of the more notable quotes remembered by Terry Blake. It was the best publicity he could have hoped for. He recalls that the Vice Squad was called in and regular newspaper vendors were warned by major newspaper publishers not to sell the *Whisper*. This had the opposite effect. The deeper their newspaper went underground, the better it sold.

NSW Police had by now worked out that charging those selling the *Whisper* would be as counter-productive as arresting the prostitutes who worked openly in Woods Lane in Darlinghurst or closing down the gambling clubs that thrived in Kings Cross. A little controlled illegality was now tolerated in the Askin era. The *Whisper* had come in at exactly the right time.

Not so in Queensland where it was banned in 1965 both for its content and the system of selling by street vendor. In April of that year, two Sydney men were charged and fined after attempting to sell copies on the streets of Melbourne. The police prosecutor said the newspaper was 'a clumsy attempt at satire and had a substantial sex content'. He said it was obscene under the dictionary definition of the word. Eventually the *Whisper* could be sold in Victoria but only after the models' nipples were deleted by airbrush. The nipple-free Victorian edition also sold in Tasmania. Adelaide proved to be a lucrative market after Blake introduced his publication by announcing on radio that he would stand on the steps of the Town Hall at noon, challenging authorities to come and arrest him. They didn't but a huge crowd bought every paper he had.

The *Whisper* was a revolutionary idea when it started but it lost its impact when it went to newsagency distribution, getting rid of the street sellers who gave it most of its original anarchic charm. The title was bought by maverick publisher Maxwell Newton in 1975, after which the actor Max Cullen describes it as 'a fairly grubby soft porn rag'. Cullen, along with his brother Fred, had been among the original contributors.

In a survey of satire in the 1960s, *Private Eye* magazine noted that the *Whisper* was the only mass-market satirical tabloid in the world, although Terry Blake never liked the word satire with its intellectual connotations. '*The Shorter Oxford*', he wrote, 'describes satire as "the employment, in speaking or writing, of sarcasm, irony, ridicule etc. in denouncing, exposing, or deriding vice, folly, abuses or evils of any kind." Fair enough, but I like the broader, Australian definition—having a go at the bastards by laughing at 'em.'

The success of *Oz* and the *Whisper* sparked a fad for underground newspapers, all trying to push the boundaries of the law that little bit further.

*Censor* magazine adopted the *Whisper* philosophy of using street vendors—the freakier the better.

The short-lived *Censor* magazine pushed a little too hard when it published a cover photo of Sandra Nelson, the stripper who had previously made the front pages of daily papers when she made her topless tour of Sydney. This time she was naked, posing on the colonnade of the NSW Supreme Court building.

The Chief Justice, Sir Leslie Herron, was recovering in hospital when he was shown the publication.

'It may be considered obscene', said Sir Les. 'At the very least it is a shocking breach of bad taste. I was greatly offended to think the Supreme Court was being used for such material.' He asked that the matter be referred to the Crown Solicitor. The magazine was also deemed offensive by Victorian legal authorities when two teenagers were arrested after selling copies on Melbourne streets.

'I believe the magazine would tend to deprave and corrupt the persons who read it', said Mr J. Moloney, SM. 'It unduly emphasises sex and comes under the definition of obscenity.'

*Censor*, and a similar publication, *Obscenity*, had previously been in trouble with the law. Detective-Sergeant Shenele of the NSW Vice Squad went on a tour of Sydney's newsagents one day in May 1966 and bought copies of *Censor* No. 2 magazine from four vendors. This edition included extracts from the novel *Fanny Hill*, then banned by Australian Customs.

'I paid 30 cents for each copy', Shenele told the Central Court in August. 'Salaskas (one of the accused news vendors) whose stand is located on the corner of Pitt and Market Streets, displayed a poster advertising *Censor* with the words "Adults Only" printed on it. The front page of the magazine was visible to members of the public.'

Copies of *Obscenity* were also openly for sale. This publication was advertised in *Oz* magazine with the warning that it had already been banned in Victoria and Queensland: 'It contains extracts from three banned books: Marquis de Sade's *Juliette*, *Kama Sutra* and *Decameron*, two pages about the four-letter word, reviews of other banned books and so much more the mind boggles.' Potential purchasers were advised that copies would be sent to them under plain wrapper … 'it's much cheaper that way'.

Six men were charged with publishing and selling these allegedly obscene magazines. In court, Mr Lewer, SM, gave a detailed account of the some of the contents of *Censor* magazine.

'There are photos of partly-clad women—pure calendar stuff, nothing lascivious, nothing lewd. There are extracts from a banned book, *Fanny Hill*, which is hard to read as it is written in an out-of-date style of journalism.'

Mr Gee (for the Crown) added further highlights.

'Page 5 of *Censor* has a column which contains what is titled "The Playboy Advisor" containing what purports to be advice of sexual matters but which puts forward a view which could offend public taste. The last page has what are known as "Playboy Party Jokes", which are in such poor taste as to offend the public. There are references to homosexual behaviour. In *Fanny Hill* a young girl watches various sexual acts which are described in very great anatomical detail. One could look in vain in our community for anything that goes as far as this does.'

The magistrate didn't agree. He determined that the extracts from *Fanny Hill* and 'The Playboy Advisor' could be described as indecent but dismissed more serious charges of obscenity, based largely on a ruling made in Ontario that *Fanny Hill* was not obscene.

'I am prepared to adopt for this community those standards that have been adopted for the Canadian community', he said.

Three men were fined $20 each with $22 costs.

Also charged with obscenity was Michael Brown, a largely unknown artist, who supported his creative career with fruit-picking and factory work.

In November 1965 he definitely made an impact.

His first major exhibition at Gallery A in Paddington, Sydney, included several paintings incorporating private parts of the male and female anatomy. Others had four-letter words painted on them in inch-high letters. One of these words was described quaintly as 'Mr Tynan's word', a reference to the English theatre critic Kenneth Tynan, the man credited with saying 'fuck' for the first time on television.

When interviewed by Frank O'Neill of Sydney's *Daily Mirror*, Michael Brown appeared to be hoping for some similar reaction to his own use of Tynan's word.

'I suppose it's just cheap sensationalism', he told O'Neill 'but even cheap sensationalism is jumping and alive and has more life in it than any of the things called art.'

He wrapped up the interview with some fashionable nihilism— 'I think you would be doing them a favour if you dropped a bomb on them', he said of Sydneysiders in general.

Then, having dangled the bait, he waited for someone to grab it. He hooked just about the biggest fish in Sydney. The next day, as if on cue, Detective Sergeant Farrell strolled into Gallery A to check out the paintings. Bumper Farrell was a legendary hard man whose reputation included biting off the ear of an opponent during his Rugby League days. Later, as a Kings Cross copper, he was renowned for taking crims down dark alleyways to administer some rough justice.

Bumper was not a noted lover of the visual arts.

'I would not claim to be an art critic', he admitted later. 'I seldom go to art shows except in the line of duty.'

His line of duty on this occasion was to determine whether Michael Brown's paintings were indecent or not. He wouldn't comment on the record, but a reporter who just happened to be there noted that the big man appeared to recoil at the sight of one work. Bumper's official report, with incriminating photos, was later sent to the Chief Secretary Mr Willis for consideration.

In December 1966 Michael Brown, then aged 28, appeared in the Number One Court of Petty Sessions. Fourteen of his paintings were hung on the courtroom walls and four of these, plus one photograph, were also on trial.

Brown was facing charges of having delivered indecent paintings to Gallery A for exhibition and with having assisted the gallery to exhibit them. The ominous presence of Gerry Locke, SM, was presiding.

As he had previously in the Land of *Oz*, Locke wanted to establish early on who was in charge here.

'As I understand the law, it is for the Court—and let's not mince words, that means me—to decide whether or not a certain matter is indecent. It seems to me that it is quite irrelevant to the consideration of that question what this witness thinks about whether a painting is indecent or not.'

The witness referred to was John Reed BA, author and one of the founders of the Contemporary Arts Society of Victoria. Reed must have been feeling an extreme sense of déjà vu. Twenty years before he was the co-editor of *Angry Penguins* when it, and his friend Max Harris, were similarly on trial.

This case would prove to be equally surreal.

Locke: 'What would you say if the artist had portrayed the anus of that man and nothing but the anus of that man; would you say that such a thing could have artistic merit?'
Reed: 'If you present me with a painting of an anus and then ask me if it had artistic merit I would be able to answer.'
Locke: 'So you mean it is possible for such a painting to have artistic merit?'
Reed: 'I say you cannot say in abstract. Show me the painting and then I could give you an answer.'

No such painting was produced. Nor was the painting of the inside of a sewer pipe which Locke also raised, questioning whether this would have artistic merit or not. Later in the proceedings the conversation turned to what appeared to be a penis.

Police prosecutor: 'Referring to different parts of the work, you see an elongated object on the bottom left corner in a mauve colour?'

The witness, Elwyn Lynn, art critic for *The Australian* and *The Bulletin*, said he could.

Police prosecutor: 'Could you form an opinion as to what

that represents?'
Lynn: 'A penis-like, worm-like object.'
Police prosecutor: 'Would you form the view that it was meant to represent a penis?'
Lynn: 'Partially.'

Later, Lynn was asked to clarify a further anatomical detail.

Police prosecutor: 'I refer you to the section in the bottom left-hand corner and referring firstly to that figure in orange—do you agree that that purports to be the figure of a female?'
Lynn: 'Yes.'
Police prosecutor: 'That the vaginal region is depicted most conspicuously?'
Lynn: 'Yes.'
Police prosecutor: 'The breasts are also depicted most conspicuously?'
Lynn: 'Well, one is a bit like a pear and one is like an apple.'
Police prosecutor: 'Have you any doubt about what they are supposed to depict?'
Lynn: 'I just simply say that they are obviously supposed to be breasts but one looks like a pear and the other like an apple.'

It made little difference in the end. Brown was handed a sentence of three months gaol with hard labour. The decision was later overturned on appeal.

One of the problems during these turbulent times was the lack of consistency of various judgements, from court to court and from state to state. In November 1967, after years of discussion, the States and the Commonwealth finally signed an agreement for a uniform censorship system. A nine-member National Literature

Board of Review was set up, taking much of the responsibility of censorship away from policemen like Bumper Farrell, not that this would have helped a visual artist like Mike Brown. Still, it appeared to be a step towards sanity and there were immediate results.

In March 1968 the Indian book of sexuality, the *Kama Sutra of Vatsayana*, went on sale throughout Australia without any fuss. This was one of the banned books included in *Obscenity* magazine. And in the same month, a Melbourne bookshop staged 'The Book Sale of the Century', including such taboo works as Vladimir Nabokov's *Lolita*, Norman Mailer's *The American Dream*, D. H. Lawrence's *Lady Chatterley's Lover*, Robert Close's *Love Me Sailor* and James Baldwin's *Another Country*. All were for sale at bargain basement prices.

And, as Keith Dunstan points out in his book *Wowsers*, they all had this in common. 'All had been banned within the past five years, and all had been subject of much controversy in Victoria. Now they were on the remainder table. Nobody cared and there was not a wowser in sight.'

Not that this was an end to the banning business. In 1968 Mr Justice Helsham of the Equity Court was asked to decide whether the November issue of *Chance* magazine was indecent or obscene, was likely to encourage depravity, and unduly emphasised matters of sex. The magazine (soft porn by today's terminology) was published in Australia but was printed in Hong Kong. On their way back into Australia, vigilant officers from the Department of Customs and Excise seized all 30 000 copies as a prohibited import. In what was described as the first case of its kind in New South Wales, Chance International Pty Ltd challenged the legality of the seizure on the basis that, as an Australian magazine, it could not be classified as a prohibited import.

This technical argument was less important to Justice Helsham than the magazine content which he described as 'a vehicle for the salacious' before dismissing the company's application.

'A general tone of dirtiness pervades the whole publication', he said, adding that he had read every word of the publication (and had also studied the pictures as well).

'The treatment of the subject matter is such that it leads to the conclusion that the magazine was produced in the knowledge the public would buy it because of some chance of finding some dirt in it.'

Deemed especially filthy were two articles under the theme of Auto Eroticism. Justice Helsham described a series of photographs of a partly-naked woman lying on her back in a car as 'simply lustful'. An eight-page comic strip called 'Barbarella' was almost incomprehensible but, according to the judge, seemed to suggest lesbianism.

On the night of Saturday 22 February, 1969, it was Phil Noyce's turn.

The future director of *Newsfront, Dead Calm* and *Rabbit-Proof Fence* was then an 18-year-old Sydney University law student living at home in leafy, upper-class Wahroongah. On Saturday night he was selling copies of the underground newspaper *Ubu News* (ten cents a copy) out front of the Hornsby Ku-ring-gai Police-Citizens Boys' Club in George Street, Hornsby. The *Ubu* collective, named after the work of anarchist playwright Alfred Jarry, had been founded in 1965 by experimental filmmakers Albie Thoms, Aggy Read, David Perry and John Clark. *Ubu News* gave details of the group's activities and philosophy, including screenings of under-ground films and what were known at the time as happenings.

Underground or not, the activities of *Ubu* would have been common knowledge to regular readers of the *Sunday Mirror* tabloid who, after a 1967 *Ubu* screening *of The Tribulations of Mr Dupont Nomore*—'an hilarious domestic fantasy'—were warned on the front page that 'TV IDOL DANCES WITH NUDE GIRLS'. The television idol was the actor Michael Boddy who appeared on ABC television programs when not busy dancing with naked girls.

Perhaps this publicity alerted Constable Phillipson of Hornsby Police when a resident brought in a copy of *Ubu News* on the following Monday. 'He showed me a drawing on page five which he considered to be filth', Constable Phillipson said. He agreed with that description.

According to documents later displayed as part of a 2004 State Records of NSW exhibition, the newspaper was then forwarded to Vice Squad Detective Sergeant V. Green (1st Class) who decided that this drawing, and a further article on page 13, were indeed obscene.

Noyce was also selling *Ubu News* in Hornsby on the following Saturday night when he was approached by another constable in plain-clothes. After confirming that pages 5 and 13 were still obscene, Noyce was asked to accompany him to the Police-Citizens Boy's Club building where Constable Phillipson was waiting.

He pointed out the drawing on page 5 to Noyce and said, 'I consider this drawing is obscene'. The cartoon featured a man wearing jeans on the top half of his body. Noyce did not reply. The constable then said, 'I am going to read part of a sentence appearing on page 13 to you which I consider to be filth and it is definitely obscene.'

Although it was now State Government policy to prosecute the publishers of a publication rather than the sellers, the Chief Secretary's department decided to proceed with this case on the grounds that Noyce was a staff member partly responsible for editing and publishing the newspaper. In February 1970, at the Central Court of Petty Sessions, the offence was found to be proved but the magistrate did not proceed to a conviction. Noyce received a $50 fine and a 12-month good behaviour bond and was ordered to pay a peppercorn payment of $2 court costs.

# chapter **twenty**

# **Full frontal**

**N**ambour-born actress Carole Skinner generally gets the credit for being the first person to appear naked on a theatrical stage in Australia.

In May 1969, as part of the Sydney University Dramatic Society's (SUDS) production of *The True History of Squire Jonathan and His Unfortunate Treasure,* she appeared as the Blonde Lady, a part that required her to undress and perform a lengthy nude scene, or to be accurate, wearing only a belt.

'I approached that part from the point of view that it really was a beautiful little role', said Carole, in real life a redhead with freckles. Thanks to her beautiful little role this play was perhaps the first SUDS production to make the front pages of the Sydney tabloids.

It placed her at the front of the nude queue ahead of all those actors (male and female) who would undress in the musical *Hair,* which began its Australian season on 5 June.

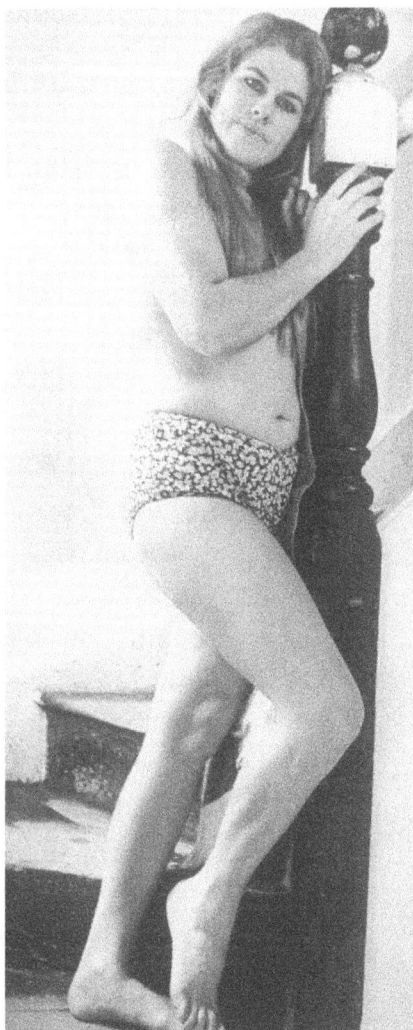

Carole Skinner appeared as the Blonde Lady, wearing only a belt.

'Nobody had thought much about it and suddenly there was all this fuss and I even began getting nasty letters', said Carole shortly afterwards. 'I got pretty upset about it, thinking nobody would ever hire me again and I'd be branded as "that girl in the nude scene".' Any misgivings disappeared a few days after the fuss when she was on her way to the corner shop and saw her front-page story lying in the gutter in the rain. 'It was a marvelous moment when I suddenly realised they'd all forgotten it.' (These days Carole is better remembered for her role as nasty Nola McKenzie in the 'Prisoner' series).

*Hair* made its debut at the art deco Metro Theatre in Kings Cross, Sydney. The producer, Harry M. Miller, cleverly promoted it as a chance for middle Australians to see what the Woodstock generation was all about. He famously described this (and another of his productions, *Boys in the Band*) as the only '100 per cent moral' pieces of theatre he had staged.

Maybe, but the fact that just about everyone on stage took off their clothes is what most people were there for. This is how the *Sydney Morning Herald*'s Margaret Jones saw the musical in her report on the front page of the newspaper.

'In the tumultuous last number of the first act of the love-rock musical *Hair*', she wrote, 'most of the cast struggled out of their clothes under cover of a tent-like sheet. The young men and women stood naked for about thirty seconds before the curtain fell. The pastel lighting was subdued but the figures were still clearly visible. Even before the mass strip began three girls, two white and one Negro, stripped to the waist in the second to last number, "Be In", and danced with bare breasts.'

The cast in the long-running series of performances of *Hair* around Australia included Reg Livermore and a teenage Marcia

Hines. The show had opened with the tacit approval of New South Wales Chief Secretary Willis, who was invited to attend a special preview. He gave it a tentative thumbs up.

> 'I cannot possibly support the way *Hair* lampoons accepted standards of morality and loudly proclaims every known vice from blasphemy and drug-taking to homosexuality and draft-dodging', he said after his preview. 'However, it is cleverly presented and quite revolutionary as a form of theatre.'

A bomb hoax on opening night was interpreted as a more damning form of criticism.

Harry Miller's other 100 per cent moral enterprise had a more troubled existence. *Boys in the Band*, the play by Matt Crowley, centres around a birthday party attended by nine openly homosexual men. Its most celebrated line, spoken by one actor as he enters the room is: 'Who do you have to fuck to get a cup of coffee round here?'

Similar language peppers the script. But in 1968, six years after Lenny Bruce was banned for using the Kenneth Tynan word, the play survived a seven-month Sydney season without one complaint.

No such luck in 1969 when the boys moved their band south of the border to Melbourne's Playbox Theatre. Sitting in the audience during the third week of performances were two Vice Squad

*Boys in the Band.*

detectives, armed with stopwatches, note pads and pencils. Three of the actors, John Krummel, Charles Little and John Norman were charged with using obscene words in a public place. Harry M. Miller shrewdly sensed a priceless publicity opportunity and decided to fight the charges in court.

One Vice Squad detective said that he had counted five indecent expressions, the first being uttered on the night in question at 8.45 p.m. The other counted seven, starting at 8.47 p.m.

The magistrate, Mr Kelly, wanted to know what these expressions were.

And so, for perhaps the first time in a Melbourne court, the second detective solemnly consulted his notes and read out: 'Fuck, fucking, cunt, shit, arsehole, supertwat and arse'.

Mr Kelly then decided he needed to see the play for himself. After his research he found the charges proved but described the offences as 'trifling'. The Victorian Crown Law Department appealed and the initial decision was overruled in the Victorian Supreme Court. Krummel and Little were each fined $25. John Norman received a lesser fine of $10. Melbourne had once again proved that it was less lenient than sinful Sydney.

During this period the director and actors of the Alex Buzo play, *Norm and Ahmed*, were also convicted of using obscene language.

Harry M. Miller continued the Melbourne season, now playing to packed houses, with the seven offending words removed. When the play

A young Henri Szeps starred as Harold in *Boys in the Band*.

returned for a second Sydney season they were re-instated, as before, without any fuss.

According to legend it was the comedian Roy Rene who first used the word F.U.C.K. on an Australian stage. He didn't say it, he spelt it out instead. In his early days on the variety circuit before the Second World War, Roy Rene was part of a very popular double act called Stiffy and Mo. One of the highlights of their show was when Mo (Roy Rene) drew a large letter F on a blackboard. He then asked his sidekick to tell him what the letter was. Stiffy would study the board carefully before answering, 'K'. Mo wiped the board clean before again printing the letter F. Stiffy studied the board even more carefully before again saying that it was the letter K. They did this a third or fourth time before, in mock frustration, Mo demanded of his partner: 'How come every time I write F you see K?'

There are some who now deny that this ever happened; that it is a theatrical myth. Mo was always considered a 'blue' comedian, although he didn't use bad language (the word 'bloody' was considered too strong for the stage). But he had a knack of making the most innocent of actions appear unspeakably obscene.

One example is provided by fellow performer Willie Fennell.

'I'll never forget when I started doing stage shows. Roy and I were both in Brisbane, and I watched him work the night before I was due to go on. His sketch before interval was a thing called 'Pearl the Sharp Shooter' and you must get a mental picture of him coming out with a horrible phallic-looking whip with a tassel on the end, and one of the ballet girls holding a banana. Roy said: 'I do all the whip cracking and I do cracks this way, that way and up that way.' What he did with the bloody banana and the ballet kid and the whip you can't imagine. It was the filthiest sketch, and the audience was killing themselves and I was thinking: "Oh, my God".'

Backstage, when Fennell went to congratulate him, Roy Rene warned him in all seriousness not to try anything blue in a family town like Brisbane. Fennell pointed out that tonight's show was the bluest he'd ever seen, something that genuinely shocked the great Mo.

'What do you mean? It's all in their minds, that's all!'

When he performed on radio, Roy Rene was forced to tone down his act.

'He had to be a bit cleaner for radio, but redoing his stuff was no real problem because even on stage he never actually said blue things', wrote former scriptwriter Fred Parsons in his biography, *A Man called Mo*. 'He never said a word a child couldn't repeat at home—it was all by inference. All his comedy was in the way he reacted to what somebody else had said.'

Even on radio, it was as if you could see what evil thoughts Mo was thinking.

In the golden era of live radio, each station would have its own censor who attended rehearsals to check that the script was suitable for public consumption. As Parsons remembers, censors would usually determine how blue a line was by how hard the cast laughed when they first heard it.

'I found out that all censors are the same; if they tell you to take out a line, they expect you to put in a clean one instead. I'd say: "Yes, Ernie", and substitute something that Roy could react to in an even bluer way.'

This system was also suggested by Actors Equity when an inquiry into the launch of television was held in 1953. How these in-house censors would respond to live-to-air telecasts was never explained. As it turned out television would be largely self-censored with the Australian Broadcasting Control Board, set up in 1949 to control radio, acting as judge and jury in extreme cases.

In 1951 when Dame Enid Lyons was appointed a member of the Australian Broadcasting Commission, she said: 'I don't care if television comes to Australia. I think I would prefer that it didn't. But it will so we must be prepared for it.' Commenting that programs must be chosen very carefully she added: 'We must never have the spectacle of women's wrestling matches on our television screens.'

The boundaries were further defined after the introduction of television when the Board advised that some 'regular program personalities have introduced jokes, comments or actions capable of bearing a double-meaning' and that 'the less desirable meaning had not been missed was made obvious by the audience.' They blamed insufficient rehearsal and ad-libbing for this disturbing tendency and warned all stations involved. Mo would have sniggered in his grave.

But from the beginning television programming rarely pushed the boundaries of bad taste for fear of offending the viewers or, more importantly, the advertisers. The usual excuse was that television was such an intimate medium, beamed directly into people's homes where ten-year-olds will be sitting in one corner while granny is knitting in the other. A memorable example of early self-censorship was of bottles of wine being removed from tables in a café scene on the 'Bandstand' show.

Sex seemed to not exist on television until 1967 when someone at TCN9 in Sydney decided that Australian audiences were ready for an 'adults only' tonight show.

Fronted by American entertainer Don Lane, the show had a definite Las Vegas feel. According to details handed out to the press in advance by Publicity Manager Franie O'Hanlon, Don would be performing with the Les Girls ballet, followed by special appearances by female impersonator Carlotta, the comedian Joe Martin (famed for his blue humour) and Kings Cross stripper Sandra Nelson. Also included, for no obvious reason, was a pre-recorded interview with Dan Blocker from the 'Bonanza' series.

It sounds like a swinging idea but the tempting program schedule is about as far as it went. The show was cancelled before it could even go to air. The mere idea of Don Lane performing with a group of dancing gender benders was enough for someone high up to can it pronto.

There were other attempts to break through the moral brick wall. ATN7 produced a television series based on Jon Cleary's novel *You Can't See Round Corners*. The subject matter was updated to include current issues like the Vietnam War, drugs and, of course, post-Pill promiscuity. A bedroom seduction scene was included featuring actress Carmen Duncan, but most of the local stations forming the Seven national network chose to delete this. In 1969 Seven made a feature film adaptation of the series which included a recreation of the missing sex scene.

# chapter **twenty-one**

# **Grubby Gra Gra**

Then there was Graham Kennedy. The King of Television was a noted opponent of censorship, especially if it related to him. But he also responded to any decision that he deemed unfair or absurd.

In 1966 a five-metre high plaster replica of Michelangelo's *David* made a tour of David Jones department stores throughout Australia. It appeared as Michelangelo originally intended except for Melbourne, where a giant fig leaf had to be added to protect the more innocent shoppers. Even posters of the unadorned statue were removed from display. Kennedy protested by showing original posters on his show and displaying another replica of the

The King of Television supported the rights of Australians to see *David* as Michelangelo intended, sans fig leaf.

statue, minus fig leaf, as made by a local admirer. He then challenged Victoria's Chief Secretary, the man responsible for censoring the most famous statue in the world, to an on-air

Face of a choirboy, mouth of a sewer, claimed his critics.

debate. 'I cannot see us getting into trouble', he told his audience. 'Mr Meagher cannot seize all the TV sets.'

Another of the King's transgressions was in 1968 during a live commercial for a new rubbish bin fitted with wheels. He joked that

COURTESY OF GTV NINE PUBLICITY

one use for it would be to 'fill it with garbage and call it "Meals on Wheels" for Italians'. He was forced to apologise after numerous calls of protest from viewers.

An official reprimand came after showing some footage of Carlton captain-coach Ron Barassi responding to the crowd at a football match. He made a few suggestions as to what Barassi might be saying, before adding: 'Actually, I don't think any of those things were right, it was some sort of request involving a taxidermist.' This comment was enough to earn a caution from the Australian Broadcasting Control Board (ABCB), which in turn sparked a life-long battle with this censorship authority.

Later, when he was cautioned for using the words 'horse's arse' on air he challenged the ABCB chairman Myles Wright to a debate on his show. This offer was not taken up.

By this time four-letter words were being heard freely on film and in the theatre although they were still illegal if spoken in other public arenas. In January 1972, rock musician Billy Thorpe (his best remembered song is 'Most People I Know Think That I'm Crazy') was charged after using the F-word on stage at Sydney's Chequers nightclub. He told the Central Court of Petty Sessions that the language he used went pretty much like this: 'I got into trouble saying fuck on the stage, so I won't say fuck any more. They told me I'd be fined $50 every time I said fuck. I'm not allowed to say fuck on radio, so fuck radio.'

Thorpie was let off with a $40 fine and a caution from the magistrate that: 'It is clear here that it was used to shock the audience and it is a clear case of obscenity for obscenity's sake.'

The magistrate was responding to comments made by Thorpe's lawyer that the same word was used ten times in the musical *Hair*, without prosecution. This case was different, the magistrate maintained. The typical *Hair* audience knew they would hear the word on stage while the audience at Chequers nightclub had not been warned of obscenity.

Nor had those viewers watching the return of King Kennedy to television in 1975.

This controversy is detailed in full in Graeme Blundell's biography, *King: The Life and Comedy of Graham Kennedy*. The King's comeback was launched by the Nine Network with all the pomp of a royal occasion. On the first 'Graham Kennedy Show' on 3 March, Kennedy introduced the first sketch by personally welcoming his old adversary, Myles Wright. That set the tone for a show that turned an increasingly deeper shade of blue.

One of the skits featured a private eye (played by Bert Newton) spying on a pair of lovers in bed who turned out to be a nun and a priest. When sprung they claimed … 'and we're not even married'.

This inspired hundreds of viewer complaints but even more protested, a thousand according to one estimate, about Kennedy's use of the word 'faaark' during a live commercial for Cedel hairspray. He later claimed that this was merely his trademark crow call, an impression he'd performed many times on air since 1965. He also pointed out that the Melbourne comedienne Mary Hardy had already dropped the F-word and hadn't been rebuked.

The Control Board didn't accept this explanation and sent a personal letter to him at GTV9 asking him to defend his actions. The Board explained in the letter that they were seriously concerned at the general level of vulgarity on the show and suspected that, much as Billy Thorpe had done, he had intentionally set out to offend public taste in order to create publicity.

Kennedy retaliated on his next show by asking the studio audience to give his critics a mass crow call. They did so with delight.

'The Australian Broadcasting Control Board is a fine board', he told the audience. 'They are made up of very nice 90-year-old men. I would like to do a rooster but I'm worried about the cock-a-doodle-do.' He then gave out the telephone numbers of the ABCB and urged viewers to contact them after the show. Two thousand did. When Kennedy refused to respond, another letter was sent to Executive Producer Peter Faiman, giving him seven days to respond.

The first show of the following week was noticeably tamer. Then, on 18 March, Kennedy was banned indefinitely from performing live. He continued, briefly, to pre-record his show until 12 days later station executives were forced to delete a savage attack on Media Minister Doug McClelland.

This segment never went to air but Graeme Blundell includes the deleted dialogue in his book.

'Senator McClelland is really copping it this week. And like most Australians I hate to kick a man when he's down. But in Doug McClelland's case, I happily make an exception. He has failed and he knows it too. Now the public knows it. The misguided minister took credit for a mythical boom in television production. There is no boom. Employment in television productions is down by over 30 per cent this year.'

And so he continued, blaming his own lack of success in the ratings on unfair competition from Academy Awards presentations, imported films and cheap television series ... 'all purchased for a few hundred dollars from the Yanks'.

Then, after yelling 'Edit Point' he demanded the instant dismissal of Senator McClelland. One former Nine executive who has seen this deleted footage (he has a significant collection of Graham Kennedy out takes) describes this monologue as a Dr Strangelove moment.

After deleting this diatribe GTV9 General Manager Leon Hill himself made an announcement before the start of the show that a segment had been removed because of 'a combination of bad taste and a cowardly attack on a person who didn't have the opportunity to reply'.

The King was Dead. Graham Kennedy quickly resigned from

Nine (a mutual decision according to insiders) and tried to grab martyrdom by claiming that 'political censorship of this sort is something you used to be shot for in Germany and Russia'.

But the real reason for his departure was far from political. After less than six weeks Kennedy had gained only half the ratings of his tonight show rival Ernie Sigley ... 'but he [Kennedy] was costing the Nine Network twice as much in salary' pointed out the columnist Veritas.

Another reason, perhaps more significant, was that Australia's King of Comedy was no longer very funny.

'The charm is no longer there', wrote the *TV Week* reviewer. 'Now, when he slips in one of his crude, oft-told jokes, he comes across as a dirty old man.'

Grubby Gra Gra, as he was now being called, returned to radio in Melbourne and turned up the smut-o-meter even higher, finally getting his public revenge on Senator McClelland by calling him 'a turd' on 3DB.

There was worse to come for those easily offended. In 1977 Graham Kennedy returned to television, this time for the fledgling 0–10 network, as host of a game show called 'Graham Kennedy's Blankety Blanks'. It was a local version of one of those 'hundred dollar Yank' shows he had slammed when they were beating him in the ratings.

Announcing the new project, the station said that it had spoken with the ABCB and been advised of its guidelines. 'We will be ready to censor anything that may be offensive.'

Whatever the guidelines were, 'Blankety Blanks' goes down in history as one of the smuttiest, and most successful, programs in television history. Towards the end of the show's year long run, even the network's General Manager Ian Kennon walked out during a taping of the show, obviously shocked by the level of smut. Even Stuart Wagstaff, the suave spokesman for Benson & Hedges cigarettes, was dropping the F-word freely. 'Blankety Blanks' was pre-recorded and needed to be. One of Gra Gra's trademarks was to mime the cutting motion of a pair of scissors after particularly crude comments from him or his guests. Some of these segments survived but most were removed as the host had predicted.

'There's nothing wrong with vulgarity if it is done well, professionally', said Kennedy in 1978. 'Vulgarity done by amateurs usually drops to the level of smut, and just becomes another dirty joke.'

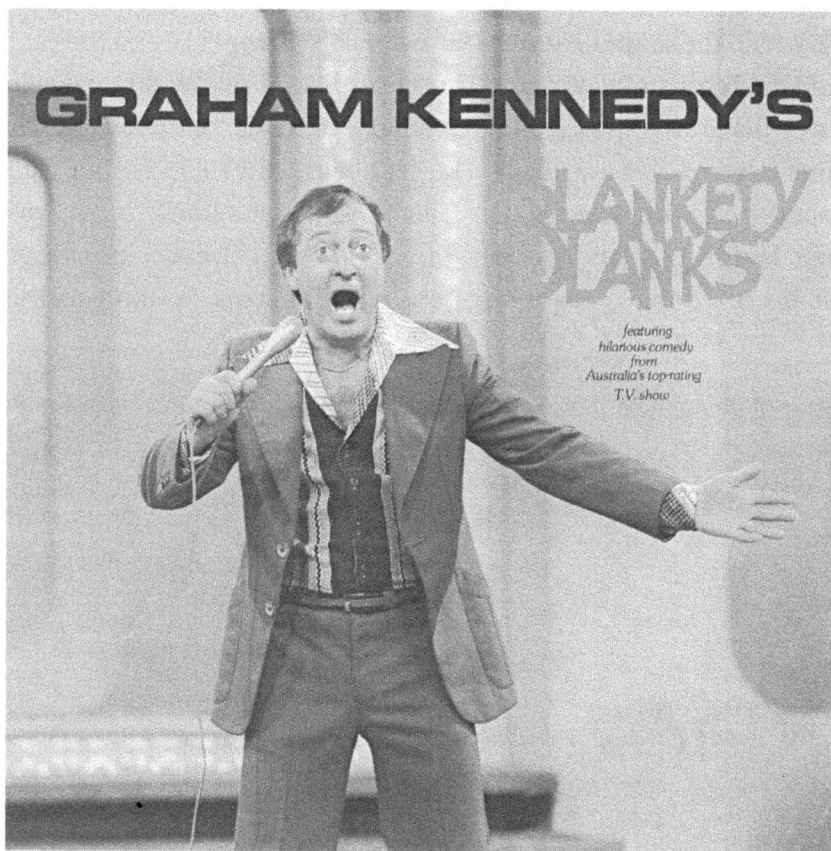

Stark reminder of Gra Gra's blue period. The highlights of 'Blankety Blanks' were released on an LP record.

# chapter **twenty-two**

# How far is too far?

**N**ineteen-seventy-two is regarded as the year in which, to use the common cliché, Australia lost its virginity. It was the year in which the soapie 'Number 96' began on Channel 10 and the year in which hirsute actor Jack Thompson, hand placed strategically over his crotch, posed for Australia's first male centrefold in the first issue of *Cleo* magazine. The year before the first sex shop had opened in Sydney and a year later Tim Burstall's movie *Alvin Purple*, featuring a smorgasbord of well-known actresses in various states of undress, was a huge box office success. So too was the

Alvin meets Abigail. The King and Queen of 70s sexuality get it together.

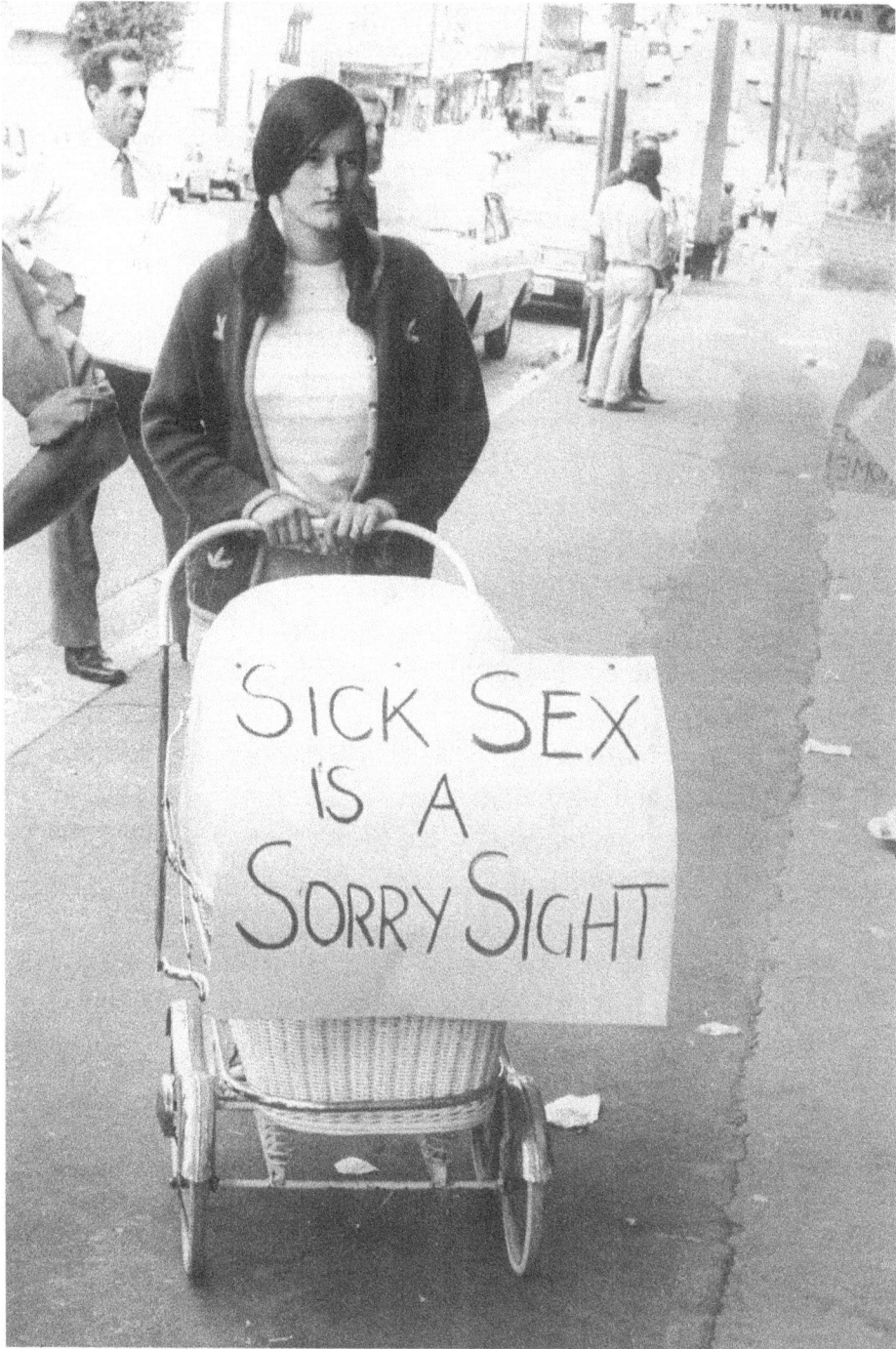

Not everyone in the 70s approved of the sexual revolution.

local release of Bernardo Bertolucci's *Last Tango in Paris*, complete with a new-fangled R certificate rating. A year before *Percy*, a quaint sex romp produced in Britain, had earned the distinction of being the first movie to be awarded an R rating by Don Chipp. These minor milestones, scattered among more substantial social movements like gay liberation and women's rights, were briefly interrupted by those opposing the new morality.

The Reverend Fred Nile became director of the Festival of Light in 1970 and commenced his crusade against all forms of whatever he deemed to be immoral. The now defunct Democratic Labor Party, fronted by Catholic conservative B. A. Santamaria, joined Nile in some campaigns, notably the attempted banning of *Last Tango*. And in February 1974 the Women's Christian Temperance Union of New South Wales wrote a stinging letter to Pat Hills MLA protesting about a new enterprise opening just a few doors down from their Sydney offices.

> 'Today on arrival at our HQ in 599 George Street we were shocked and dismayed to see a signwriter preparing the window of a premises at No. 603 George Street for what is obviously to be a "sex shop", or suppliers of pornographic material.'

It was the 1970s in a nutshell. The group that had been nobly struggling to prevent cigarette smoking and alcoholic consumption at the dawn of the twentieth century were now threatened with a window display of vibrators and inflatable dolls. For the record, their complaint was treated seriously enough for the Vice Squad to take photos of the offending premises and place them in their files.

These surveillance photos were among the highlights displayed recently at an exhibition at the NSW State Records office. Along with confiscated porno literature like *Triple Treat Woman* and *House of Lust* (both published by Down Under Classics of

Cammeray and both still on the restricted list) are less offensive items like a copy of Skyhooks 'Guilty Until Proven Insane' record album—six songs were banned from radio play, including 'Why Dontcha All Get Fucked'— and a small tin badge bearing the slogan 'Let's Lock Loins'. This was considered obscene enough for some outraged citizen to hand it in.

The offending Skyhooks album. Six songs were considered unfit for radio airplay.

'Number 96' and 'The Box' are frequently quoted as the raunchiest television series from the swinging seventies. The launch of 'Number 96' on 14 March 1972, inspired a rash of angry phone calls to Channel 10 headquarters in Sydney and other states. Most said that the show was depraved and disgusting but a Ten spokesperson made an interesting observation based on conversations with the two switchboard operators on duty that night. All those who phoned to complain did so during the commercial breaks.

While 'Number 96' showed breasts and buttocks and referred coyly to homosexuality, Satanism and the use of inflatable dolls, 'The Box' went further, giving Australian viewers its first lesbian kiss. 'The Box' remains one of the first television series to be the subject of a public protest. The Festival of Light, which had previously concentrated on films and theatrical productions like *O Calcutta!*, considered this series wicked enough to be included in their Hall of Shame.

But it was good old Aunty ABC which produced a television series that was more explicit than either of the above two. 'Alvin Purple', launched in 1976, was based on the two, hugely successful *Alvin Purple* movies produced and directed by Tim Burstall. Each episode began with the warning. 'Viewers are warned that past this point naked persons are about to be encountered. You have three seconds …' Naked persons, male and female, were encountered in abundance.

It was a wonderfully silly series, written by Alan Hopgood and starring the aforementioned Graeme Blundell as the irresistible Alvin. Also appearing were Chris Haywood as his less-successful mate Rod, plus just about every actress in Australia who was willing to strip for the camera. In one episode, Alvin receives a buck's night gift of six girls, all naked, who are sitting on the couch waiting for him to return home. When he does, they carry him off to bed. In the morning the girls, still naked, are seen forming a queue outside the toilet. This may have been the first time genteel ABC viewers saw glimpses of pubic hair on their screens.

The public reaction was as expected, but 13 episodes were filmed and screened.

It was a time when television writers were seeing how far they could go without being stopped by censors. 'The Norman Gunston Show', also on ABC TV, featured a send-up soap called 'The Checkout Chicks'. On one of these segments, one of the main characters is kidnapped leaving behind only a pair of knickers. These were handed to one of her workmates who casually sniffed them and then said, 'yes, they're hers'.

Bill Harding, the writer of this segment, told me many years later that he is still amazed that this scene sneaked through uncut. He said with some pride that this was probably the most outrageous thing he'd ever seen on mainstream television. Certainly it's hard to imagine the panty-sniffing scene, or even one featuring six naked women on a couch, being allowed in the current commercial television climate.

In the 1970s there was something in the air that encouraged all this—even on the nightly news. Now part of television mythology is the famous 'stripper' weather girl featured by Channel Ten in Adelaide at the end of their prime-time bulletin. She didn't exactly strip but would appear in either a bikini or mini-skirt, sometimes with see-through top or blouse unbuttoned to the waist. Hers was a non-speaking role and her identity was kept a secret. As the newsreader gave the weather details, her job was to point out the various highlights on a weather map cleverly designed so that she would have to stretch up to reach 'tropical Darwin' or bend over to indicate the 'map of Tasmania'. A second camera provided close-ups. It was all done in the cheeky style of a Benny Hill sketch and, as hard as it may be now to believe, was not a figment of my fertile teenage imagination. I've checked—it actually happened—although to my knowledge no tapes have survived.

These examples were counterbalanced by equal and opposite examples of television networks behaving traditionally. In 1978 four Brisbane girls formed the nucleus of Chicks Incorporated, described as a theatrical funk band. They recorded, to my knowledge, only the one obscure single, '(You've Got To) Jive To Stay Alive'.

The song remains less memorable than their gimmick of appearing on stage in corsets, chains, stockings and suspender belts. A video clip of the band in their stage gear was banned by Channel Seven's 'Sound Unlimited' music show because producer Graham Webb thought it unsuited to the show's G-rated Saturday morning slot. Webb said he vetoed the clip mainly because of the opening shot—a 15-second close-up of 'a woman's crotch in bikini pants swaying in the breeze'.

The owner of the crotch, drummer Miriam Curtis, complained that many television commercials were more provocative than her band's video. 'You can see half naked people selling all kind of

'We have Mike to thank for the break', said Chicks Incorporated, before packing up their lingerie and leaving Australia.

things right through the day', she said, possibly referring to a controversial ad for Razzamatazz pantihose where a girl's skirt is ripped off at a busy city intersection by a passing motorcyclist. Webb kept to the moral high ground and the Chicks Incorporated clip only appeared on television, heavily edited, on Mike Willesee's tabloid news program.

The free publicity granted by Willesee resulted in an offer from an American promoter. 'We have Mike to thank for the break', said Miriam before she and the other corporate chicks left for Hawaii. A banning in Australia was the best publicity any performer could wish for even if, in the case of Chicks Incorporated, it came to nothing.

There was still censorship in the cinema, but only under extreme circumstances. After previously fighting to allow the inclusion of films like *Woman of the Dunes* (1965), *A Blonde in Love* (1966) and *I Love, You Love* (1969) the director of the Sydney Film

Festival, David Stratton, decided to accept the decision of the chief censor when he banned Pier Paolo Pasolini's 1976 film, *Salo*. Based on the Marquis de Sade's *120 Days at Sodom*, the film included depictions of torture, vaginal and anal intercourse performed on children, and scenes in which victims were forced to eat faeces and drink urine.

It helped that *Salo* had already been universally condemned overseas. 'It is a sordid, degenerate concept of humanity', wrote Gene Moskowitz in *Variety*, and no one disagreed too strongly with Stratton's call.

In 1977 Stratton made another decision to screen the uncut version of Nagisa Oshima's erotic thriller *In the Realm of the Senses*, having received an assurance from the government that they wouldn't interfere. 'But I remember when I announced it', said Stratton, 'I received a call from the chief censor, Richard Prowse, who said it [Stratton's announce-ment] was a bit of a provocation'.

The uncut version was shown first at the Melbourne Film Festival where one woman was so distressed she had to be helped from the cinema. Prowse ordered cuts to be made and the uncut version wasn't shown in Australia for another 20 years.

The boundaries were also being tested on early afternoon television, although not always intentionally. In September 1980 those sitting down to watch Channel Seven's matinee movie, *White Comanche*, would have spilt their cups of tea and Iced Vo-Vos when they heard hostess Barbie Rogers warmly welcome them, hope

**BANNED BARBIE SAYS: I WAS SET UP**

they enjoyed the movie then add, 'and if you don't, I'll rip your tits off'. After the switchboard jammed with complaints, Barbie was suspended for a week by Seven's general manager Ted Thomas, even after the announcer explained that her segment had been pre-recorded ten days before.

'I often joke with the crew', she told *The Sun*'s John Hanrahan. 'It helps everyone relax but I don't understand how what I said went to air. Perhaps someone was trying to pull a joke on me.'

The joke was that in 1980 what was described by the station as 'unseemly language' was still punishable by a week's suspension when the same language and worse was being freely used at night. Seven was forced to issue another apology that year when a segment of a pornographic movie interrupted their telecast of the Australian Open tennis tournament.

In the same year Helen D'Amico became Australia's best-known streaker when she ran onto the ground at the Melbourne Cricket Ground Grand Final. She was fined $100, claiming in court that it was an act of impulse and she was very sorry. That was before a newspaper revealed that she was now on a very well-paid nation-wide tour as a stripper. This incident forced television networks to decide that they would no longer televise footage of streakers if they interrupted a sporting event.

# Chapter **twenty-three**

# **This is too far**

**T**elevision networks have always been notoriously nervous about their presenters' private lives, especially children's hosts and newsreaders, who are generally expected to behave like either monks or nuns. God forbid that they should behave as scandalously as do the characters in sitcoms or night time soaps. There are a multitude of examples of the double-standard at work.

'I was told my appearance wasn't in keeping with the image of a "Romper Room" teacher' said Judy-Ann Garland, better known as Miss Judy to hordes of 1970s pre-schoolers when, in 1973, she was asked to hand in her Mr Doo Bee hand puppet. Fremantle International, the producers of Channel Seven's 'Romper Room', sacked her after they disapproved of her guest appearance on a late night variety special from the Wrest Point Casino in Hobart. On this occasion she was wearing a dress that *Daily Mirror* showbiz reporter Matt White described as giving a 'peek a boo glimpse of bosom'.

White knew from personal experience that this dress, revealing as it was, was a lot more than what Miss Judy sometimes wore in the evenings. Shortly after her sacking, Matt White revealed via his column that she had paraded topless when he attended a showbiz party at her Paddington apartment.

'The party was really swinging at about 1 a.m. and I was dancing in the middle of the sitting-room, along with several others', Judy explained. 'I was wearing a very low-cut jacket and no bra underneath. Suddenly, one of the men said, "get your gear off". So I did.'

She spent the rest of the evening topless, most noticeably while handing out drinks to her 50 guests, many from the television

Naughty Miss Judy and nice Mr Do Bee.

industry. Her behaviour, she added, was nothing out of the ordinary.

'It was hot', she explained. 'And besides I'm quite uninhibited about that sort of thing, and I'm likely to shed ALL my gear if I'm in the mood, no matter where I am. What's wrong with going topless to a party anyway?'

There's a lot wrong with it, according to Fremantle International, if you happen to be the host of a kid's show. Miss Judy's television career seems to have ended at this point.

In the late 1990s a much-copied videotape was going around the industry, supposedly showing a then well-known female newsreader having sex in a lift with two men. The tape had been recorded by CCTV security cameras. The rumour was that it was filmed in a lift at her place of work, probably without her knowledge.

True or not, the newsreader suddenly disappeared from her slot and, to my knowledge, has never worked in television since. Odd, considering she was being promoted by the network as 'the next Jana Wendt'.

This is a classic case of discrimination as well as hypocrisy. How fascinating it would have been had the anonymous newsreader, or the more public Miss Judy, decided to take their respective employers to court for unfair dismissal. What stories they could have told about the behaviour, in lifts and at private parties, of male television personalities or senior executives.

There appears to have been a shift in attitude in the mid nineties. In 1992 a program called 'Naughtiest Home Video Show', hosted by Doug Mulray, was canned by Channel Nine, this time while on air. The show featured adults-only home video footage, including dogs and cats attempting to mate with other animals, men on a beach with flaming toilet paper jammed between their buttocks, a woman with a man's head squeezed between her breasts, a child touching a kangaroo's genitals and a couple seen in the background making love on the bonnet of their car. This sequence, about half way through the hour special, was interrupted by a blank screen and an announcement that the network was experiencing 'technical difficulties'. An episode of the sitcom 'Cheers' was shown instead.

The rumour was that Kerry Packer, boss of the Nine Network, had been watching at home and had personally ordered the show to be stopped immediately, using the memorable phrase 'Get this [expletive deleted] off air'. It seems unlikely that anyone else would have had that power.

While there were a number of complaints to television stations around Australia on the night, a large percentage were by viewers enjoying the show and wondering why it had been stopped—as many as 80% according to one source. The Australian Broadcasting Tribunal received 185 official complaints, 111 from viewers who found it disgusting, the rest by those complaining about it being axed. The ABT decided that the program did not breach its guidelines for viewing in an adults-only timeslot.

# NAUGHTY MULRAY LAUGHS AT BAN

Uncle Doug realised that being taken off air was a great career move.

Doug Mulray found the controversy amusing at the time. 'When you think of [the drama series] "Chances" and some of the stuff that goes to air, it was a seaside postcard of a show', he told the *Telegraph Mirror* a week later. 'It was rude but it was not in any way dangerous or damaging. I mean, after the *Sex* program's clitorises and genitals warts, I frankly felt it wasn't offensive.'

It was in this transition period that the unthinkable happened.

Richard Neville, the former *Oz* editor who was himself a serial victim of censorship, came out in support of the institution. In 1993 he declared that Peter Greenaway's movie *The Cook, The Thief, His Wife and Her Lover* was 'a good reason to maintain censorship'.

In 1996 he attempted to defend his initial reaction in *The Age* newspaper, revealing that he had been branded a 'squeamish wimp' by some critics. It was the violence of the film—'sado chic' as he called it—that had offended him.

'Its violence took me by surprise', he wrote 'and I felt betrayed by the critics who had extolled the painterly images, the sets and the music, without mentioning the cannibalism or child torture.'

Other films, notably those made by Quentin Tarantino, also fitted into the 'violence is cool' genre which Neville, for one, thought had gone too far.

This shift in attitude was reflected in other areas. The most memorable examples of celebrity censorship in this period are of television and sporting personalities reacting against undesirable images of themselves.

In 1993 newsreader Anne Fulwood, then working for Channel Ten in Sydney, won a legal action against the Australian edition of *Penthouse* magazine in the NSW Supreme Court. Her complaint was over a caricature which appeared in the June edition, part of a series known as 'Kantor's Celebrity Skins'. In this drawing she was depicted reading the news naked (or to be specific, naked below the news desk). A sign next to her reads News Flash.

The copy of the cartoon that I've seen shows what appears to be a minimal pair of panties but this fine black line was not raised in court. Instead, Gem Kilt, publishers of Australian *Penthouse*, decided to apologise for the 'hurt and distress' caused to Ms Fulwood, and agreed to recall and destroy as many copies of the magazine as possible. Easier said than done as the June edition was already on sale in most newsagents and, once the verdict was publicised, selling fast.

The artist Frants Kantor also apologised to Ms Fulwood, explaining that no previous celebrities had been offended by his caricatures. He added that several previous subjects had asked to buy the original artwork.

What could have amounted to one of Australia's most fascinating obscenity trials ended with a fizzle.

'I took action and as a result, the caricature will be removed from the publication and a public apology was read out in court', she said afterwards. When asked if this would be the end of the controversy, she said that it was.

Also a winner in court was Rugby League footballer turned television presenter Andrew Ettingshausen (sometimes known as ET) who successfully sued *HQ* magazine in 1993 after it featured a photo of him taking a shower during a Kangaroos tour of England. The photo was printed without his consent in the April 1991 edition published by Kerry Packer's ACP empire.

The scenario was similar in some respects to a 1978 controversy in which South Sydney Rugby League captain Darrell Bampton was shown naked and full frontal during a segment on Channel Seven's 'The Big League', filmed in the dressing rooms before a match.

Ironically, this program was hosted by Rex Mossop, the same man who protested so vehemently against nude men walking In front of his Reef Beach house. The same man who had complained about male genitals being thrust down *his* throat.

'It went to air in prime viewing time and my family has suffered a great deal because of it', said Bampton, who claimed he was unaware he was being filmed at the time and was shocked when the segment went to air, unedited, about one and a half hours afterwards. The matter reached the Supreme Court where Channel Seven expressed its regrets to Bampton and to the South Sydney club.

Although the NSW Rugby League refused to place a blanket ban on cameras in dressing rooms, television crews were asked to warn players before they started filming and this policy still applies today.

In his more recent court case, Andrew Ettingshausen took a different approach. He claimed that he had been defamed by *HQ* magazine. He said that since the magazine was published he had been constantly insulted by strangers in public and by spectators at matches.

'I hear comments continually when I am playing Rugby League', he claimed in court. 'They shout out: "Hang your cock out, ET" or "Show us your prick"… Every game I play I usually hear something of that nature.'

He also said he was distressed by 2JJJ commentators Roy and HG calling him 'the nudist' in their broadcasts.

Ettingshausen was initially awarded \$350 000 in damages. This was later reduced to \$100 000 after an appeal by ACP.

Although this court case was for defamation, not obscenity, the question of whether the shower photograph was pornographic or not was hotly debated, with the then editor of *HQ*, Shona Martyn, being subjected to a surreal grilling that reads like a Marx Brothers script.

Asked by defence barrister Ian Callinan if she regarded the photograph as sexually explicit, Shona Martyn replied: 'No.' Or pornographic? 'Certainly not', she replied. When asked she said she would not mind if a similar photograph of her appeared in a magazine.

In response, Ettingshausen's lawyer, Tom Hughes QC, decided to be more specific. He asked Shona Martyn if the photo showed his client's penis.

'I don't think it does', she replied.

Questioned further she suggested: 'There's a shadow there

which I agree that it could be construed as being Mr Etting-shausen's penis.'

Hughes asked her if she agreed with this analysis.

'I don't think reasonably', she said. 'I have been struggling to look at it, and I did not see it at the time. I mean, here I can see some shadow.'

'It is not a shadow is it?' suggested Hughes. 'It's a white shape with what looks like pubic hairs.'

After Shona Martyn disagreed with this interpretation, Hughes offered a revision.

'Well, an off-white shape. It is the shape of a penis, is it not?'

Shona Martyn said she was not certain. Hughes snapped back: 'Well, what could it be?'

'I guess it could be a shadow', she offered.

'Is it a duck?'

'I don't think it would be a duck', replied Ms Martyn.

After a second trial the award for damages was reduced to a mere $100 000. Robert Pullan, author of *Guilty Secrets: Free Speech and Defamation in Australia*, commented on the ET saga for *The Australian* newspaper.

'What made the difference between jury one and jury two?' he pondered. 'When jury one bent to their indelicate inspection of the *HQ* magazine photograph, no smile lit any of the four faces. Jury two was evidently more inclined to smile at the idea of the defamatory appendage.'

It was regarded at the time that Andrew Ettingshausen regained his reputation but ended up seriously out of pocket.

'Only the lawyers have won', summed up Pullan.

Both the Anne Fulwood and ET court cases need to be placed in context. The 1990s was a time of celebrity nude calendars, amateur strip nights and The Hellfire Club—a nightclub where fashionable young S&M enthusiasts performed in public. It seemed that anything was permissible. In this atmosphere, both *Penthouse* and *HQ* probably felt they had the right to show whatever they liked. These two court cases proved otherwise.

Even in the world of art, where everything usually is permissible, there were indications that a limit had been reached.

From the mid 1970s, the Sydney-based artist Nigel Thomson had been painting dramatic, disturbing images in a style described as critical realism (he once jokingly claimed he was the only member of the psycho-enigmatic school). His *Mother Drowning Son* (1976) is an example of his dark humour. Another work from this period shows a family posed in a typical kitchen setting beneath the advertising-style headline, 'This Family Has Just Eaten Human Flesh'. *The Burning Question* (1979) shows a man on fire in a suburban street being filmed, and interviewed, by a television news crew.

Not everyone found these images amusing. Art critic Ted Snell, reviewing Thomson's 1982 exhibition at the Quentin Galleries in Perth, described the subject matter as 'an unpleasant mixture of violence, callousness, insanity, terror and anxiety.'

In 1983 Nigel Thomson won the prestigious Archibald Prize for a sensitive portrait of wheelchair-bound art dealer Chandler Coventry, whose gallery staged the next exhibition by the artist in 1984. By this time, suggests *Australian Financial Review* art critic John McDonald, his work had taken on 'a new and savage aspect'. He took images from hard-core pornography and nudist magazines to create works that would have left even Ted Snell speechless.

*Frightened Girl* (1983–84) shows a pre-pubescent girl standing naked, and apparently under threat, in a corner of a room. In *Children's Rites* (1981–82) a group of naked children are dancing around a bound and gagged man, with an obvious erection. What makes these and other works even more disturbing, and powerful, is their veneer of innocence. The initial shock value is diluted by the

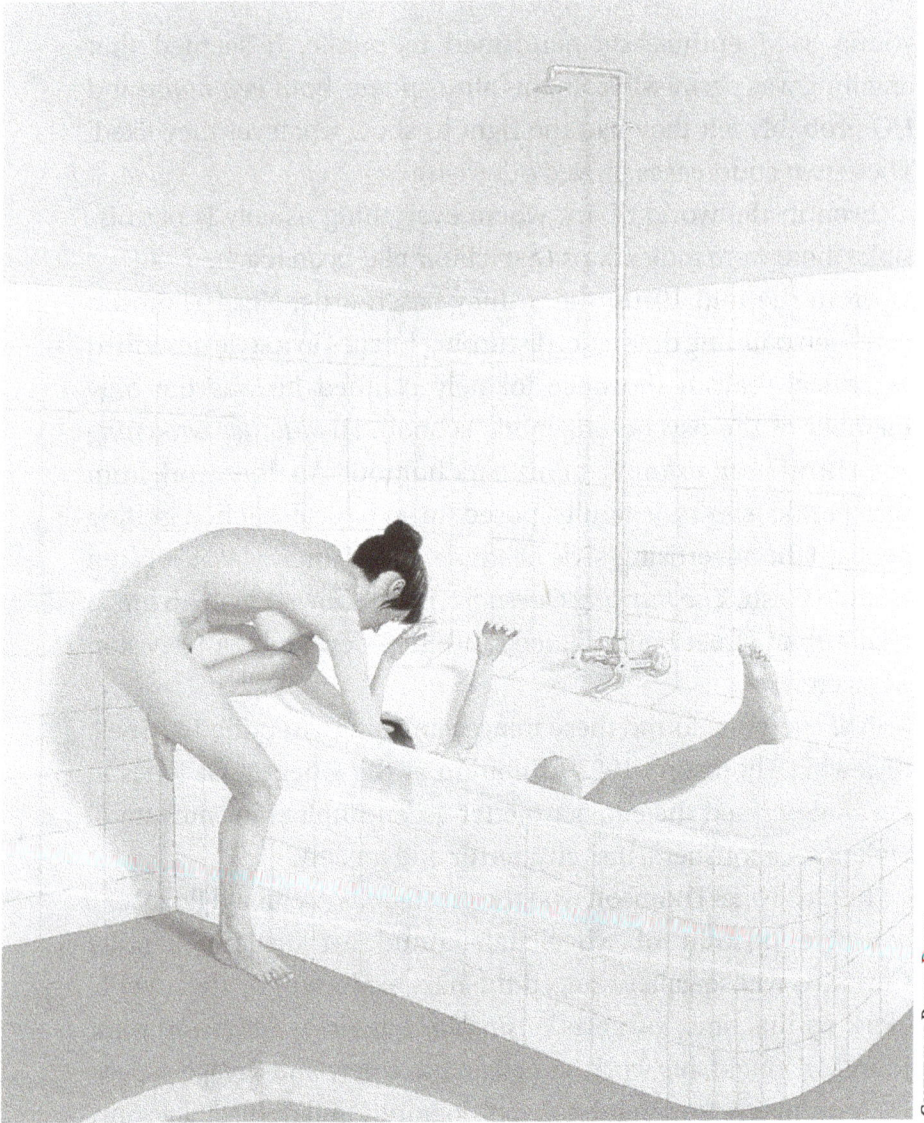

Black humour: Nigel Thomson's 1976 work, *Mother Drowning Son.*

fact that they are, as with all Thomson's work, beautifully painted.

Still, this was possibly the first time an erect penis had appeared in mainstream art and a reaction was inevitable, even in the liberal atmosphere of 1984. Thomson entered *Children's Rites* for that year's Sulman Prize (for subject painting) at the Art Gallery of NSW and the judge, Arthur Boyd, considered it worthy to be displayed. The gallery director and trustees thought otherwise and, fearing public outrage (it was, they pointed out, school holidays) withdrew the work after it had been listed in catalogue. One of those trustees, the painter Judy Cassab, later explained her decision in her auto-biography. 'Although censorship in art is abhorrent, I couldn't defend this painting with its sado-masochistic connotations connected to child pornography'.

Or perhaps that was the convenient excuse. Thomson himself suspected that the risk of losing precious private funding was the major factor in the gallery's final decision. He blamed the rise of the Moral Majority (which in Australia was spearheaded by Fred Nile's Festival of Light movement) for what appeared to be a change in attitude by the major galleries. In 1981 it was Nile who had complained about Juan Davila's painting *Stupid as a Painter*, which featured graphic images of male and female genitalia. That work was seized by the NSW Vice Squad before Premier Neville Wran—'Wran's Our Man' leaps into action again—ordered the painting be returned to public view with a token R-rating.

After the initial sting of rejection had worn off, Nigel Thomson embarked on a new series of paintings based on his experience as a young man working in a mental institution. These were equally confronting but with less obvious sexual references. The irony was that one of these works, which even the artist had considered unsaleable, was entered in the 1986 Sulman Prize and shared first prize with a painting by Wendy Sharpe. Thomson won a second Archibald Prize for his portrait of Barbara Blackman in 1997.

What Nigel Thomson had inadvertently discovered was that even in a world that could increasingly accept graphic depictions of hetero and gay sex, the mere suggestion of child pornography was taboo and was increasingly becoming a subject of concern. Even noted liberals like Phillip Adams were remarking on the 'escalation of nastiness' in art, especially violent movies.

What commentators were saying was not necessarily that these works should be censored, but that artists should have some sense of social responsibility. In other words, works of art should at least make some concession to the world that existed outside of galleries, or movie theatres, rather than operating under their own code which, in some cases, meant no rules at all. Case in point. At the 1996 Sydney Biennale, 12 videos by Austrian performance artist Hermann Nitsch were taken away for review and given an M classification. One of these videos showed a cow carcass being disembodied and a man sitting in the rib cage while entrails and blood were poured over his head.

In 1994 the Australian playwright Stephen Sewell weighed in with his own complaint against the complainants. He had written a play, *Dark Parts*, dealing with pederasty and child murder but knew that it would never be performed in the current climate. 'We couldn't even get a cast', he said. 'The actors wouldn't do it.' Yet in the same year a show called Gay Art at Sydney's Roslyn Oxley Gallery featured images of explicit male sex acts. If morality can be trivialised as operating in a similar way to fashion, gay sex was the flavour of the month while pederasty was something nobody wanted to be seen wearing.

# Chapter **twenty-four**

# **Morality for the new millennium**

**T**he challenge for those who determine morality today, and that includes every parent of a young child, is to try and control the new technology that provides unlimited access to pornography of all kinds. Any 12-year-old child has the computer knowledge to seek out hard-core imagery or can have an intimate chat over any number of phone sex lines. In a way censorship has turned full circle. Just as it was before officialdom stepped in to try and decide what we could see and do, we are now forced by access to new technology to set our own moral standards.

The limits are now nearly impossible to enforce, unless by personal choice.

An example. In April 2004, a 57-year-old dentist was charged after a witness allegedly saw him taking photos with his digital camera up the skirts of two women in a Sydney food court. The witness alleged that the dentist approached one woman from behind, placed the camera between her knees and took a shot without her noticing. He later attempted to do the same with a 15-year-old schoolgirl.

With conventional camera technology police would have been able to seize the camera and confiscate the film. But by the time police made their arrest, the man had either sent off any photo images to a computer or had erased them. At his court case the police were unable to tender any incriminating photos and Magistrate Pat O'Shane, while admitting that the man's behaviour seemed suspicious, dismissed the charges due to lack of evidence.

The internet is equally hard to control.

In July 2004, a 17-year-old student at the exclusive Barker College in Sydney was suspended after 'sexually suggestive' images of her were posted on her website and then transferred to current and former students as far away as London. The girl, a part-time model, insisted she had not been involved in posting the initial image although she later defended her actions under her web name Tahitian Temptress.

> 'I got suspended from school on Thursday—not so smart but hey when you fuck up you got to deal with the consequences don't you … anyway all I did was take a photo of myself in my school uniform in what the school called a 'compromising position'—big deal I was showing my bra, having a bit of fun.'

Even when limits can be enforced, today's media exhibits a curious form of self-censorship based, so it seems, on some insight into their readers' moral sensibilities.

At the same time as thousands of women who are not professional models appear voluntarily full frontal in the 'Home Girls' section of *The Picture* magazine, bare breasts are apparently taboo in *Who* magazine.

In *Who's* 16 June 2003 issue, a story appeared about the singer Carnie Wilson shedding 69 kilos and celebrating her weight loss by appearing as a *Playboy* centerfold. The accompanying photo appears with a patch over her breasts bearing the slogan: 'We've spared you the details'. In other words, the same bits that were shown in the pages of the *Australian Women's Weekly* in 1977 are now being banned by *Who*. You work it out.

Television is equally mysterious. Jerry Springer's television show, featuring the tabloid confessions of transsexuals, prostitutes and strippers, used to appear on the lunchtime slot when it was shown on a large screen at my local post office. Pixillation, television's equivalent to the airbrush, covered the more forbidden areas of flesh and the more offensive words were bleeped out, to the point where the show had the surreal feel of abstract art with a cartoon soundtrack.

'Neighbours', Australia's longest-running soap, introduced its first openly gay character in 2004. Lana Crawford, played by actress Bridget Neval, kissed Sky Mangel, played by Stephanie McIntosh, around 30 years after the first scenes of lesbian passion were shown on 'The Box'. Gay male couples are equally accepted, and are a mandatory inclusion on each series of 'The Block'. The first series, featuring Gav and Wazza, attracted mild criticism from radio commentators who suggested that some Australians resented having to explain homosexuality to their children. It didn't seem to matter. The final episode of the first series attracted Australia's biggest-ever television audience.

Films are also still being banned, although it is sometimes unclear where the banning stops and the shameless promotion begins. In 2003 *Ken Park*, a film which included depictions of minors having sex, was banned from screening at the Sydney Film Festival. A group calling themselves Free Cinema organised a well-publicised screening of the movie on DVD at Balmain Town Hall which was stopped when police intervened. The DVD was handed over. The ban was supported by veteran morals campaigner Fred Nile, now an MP and leader of the Christian Democrats party. Said Fred: 'If teenage actors portray under-16-year-olds in nude, explicit sex and suicide scenes … it is legally child pornography.'

The absurdity of the situation was soon pointed out. Again technology made the dispute largely meaningless. Copies of the DVD could easily be downloaded from the internet by those wanting to watch it. While Margaret Pomeranz, president of the Australia Film Critic Circle, gave it 'four stars' most other reviewers were less generous.

'Personally I just wish they hadn't banned it because then I wouldn't have had to see it', said Jonathan Biggins on ABC TV's 'Critical Mass' program. He was not the only one to suggest that without it being used for a game of moral football, the film would have passed by without anyone noticing.

A year later another movie, Catherine Breillat's *Anatomie De L'enfer* (*Anatomy of Hell*)—again featuring 'live' sex—was promoted largely on the distributor's expectation that it would be banned.

'Art or Porn? Sydney adults be the judge—while you still can' ran one typical ad. While this approach initially helped its box office, the Classification Review Board refused to take the bait. It decided to retain the R 18-plus rating and ordered more explicit advice be added to warn consumers that the film included 'actual sex, high-level sex scenes and high-level themes'.

It all seemed silly at a time when X-rated movies—featuring nothing but 'live' sex—are freely available by mail-order in Australia and are widely seen by adults in their own homes.

'The distributor of that film [*Anatomy of Hell*] specialises in taking films that are likely to be banned essentially as a marketing ploy', claimed one industry figure, anonymously quoted in the *Sydney Morning Herald*. 'The interest generated is often men in raincoats.' The men in raincoats analogy seems strangely dated in these times when people no longer have to wander out of their houses to watch erotic movies.

Again the most sensible response to this controversy came from Jonathan Biggins, this time writing in his 'don't get me started' column in *Good Weekend* magazine.

'What I want to know is, why are we so often called upon to defend such feeble films. Censorship is a serious issue. Can't someone make a really good movie that offends Fred Nile or the Concerned Wives' Association of South Australia so we can go in to bat for a quality product? The best way to make *Anatomy of Hell* disappear without trace is to let people see it.'

It's an attitude shared by most adults, although the apparent rise in the Family First movement could see some future attempts to toughen censorship laws. The current situation in which people are warned of any explicit content seems to be working well enough for most.

In other areas, the limits are less clear.

In November 2004, Peter Mackenzie, a 25-year-old builder, was arrested after secretly taking photos of topless women on Coogee beach using his video phone camera. One sunbather, and her partner, objected to having her photo taken and called the police. At Waverley Local Court, the same venue that 50 years ago had deliberated over the brevity of bikinis, Mackenzie was handed down a $500 fine, banned from any beach in the Waverley area while carrying photographic equipment, and had his video phone confiscated. The determining factor in this case was the 'clear, offended reaction of witnesses' once they realised their privacy had been invaded.

Mackenzie had transgressed the unwritten code of the beach by taking photos without consent and appeared repentant, saying he regretted his actions. 'I don't want to have a national reputation as a sleazebag', he said 'because that wasn't my intention'. This is, or was, a legally grey area. Unauthorised photos of celebrities sunbathing or swimming topless, taken by the paparazzi, appear regularly in supermarket tabloids under the generally accepted rule that a beach is a public place. Perhaps not for much longer.

This case may have inspired the proposal by the NSW branch of the Federation of Parents and Citizens' Associations in January 2005, to force parents to seek permission in writing from schools before taking photos of their children at swimming carnivals, school plays and similar events. Under the proposed guidelines parents could only photograph their own children.

By this stage some councils had already placed limitations on photography at their facilities. Parramatta City Council had a general policy described by a spokesman: 'No dirty old man in a raincoat is able to take videos, or general photographing of children, at a school carnival, or otherwise'.

While Sharyn Brownlee of the P&C Association put it less bluntly—'parents have a right to know who is videotaping or photographing their child, and schools have a responsibility of enforcing this'—the proposal was seen as unworkable, even by the most protective of parents.

In February, after community protest, Randwick City councilors reversed their intention to introduce the ban in swimming centres in their local government area.

'It's political correctness gone mad', said the manager of one pool.